Teaching Young Playwrights

Gerald Chapman

Edited and Developed
by Lisa A. Barnett

Heinemann
Portsmouth, New Hampshire

Heinemann Educational Books
361 Hanover Street, Portsmouth, NH 03801-3959
Offices and agents throughout the world

The following have generously given permission to reprint material in this book:

Pages 16–18: From "The Arbor" in *Rita, Sue and Bob, Too* by Andrea Dunbar.
Published by Methuen London. Reprinted by permission of the publisher.

Page 32: From "I'm Tired and I Want to Go to Bed" by David Torbett. Reprinted by
permission of the author.

Pages 37–38: From "Half Fare" by Shoshana Marchand in *The Young Playwrights
Festival Collection*, Avon, 1983. Reprinted by permission of the author.

Pages 70–71: From Starters developed by the Creative Arts Team. Courtesy of
Creative Arts Team/New York University.

Page 108: From "So What Are We Gonna Do Now?" by Andrea Dunbar in *The
Young Playwrights Festival Collection*, Avon, 1983. Reprinted by permission of the
author.

Every effort has been made to contact the copyright holders for permission to reprint
borrowed material. We regret any oversights that may have occurred and would
be happy to rectify them in future printings of this work.

Library of Congress Cataloging-in-Publication Data
Chapman, Gerald, b. 1949.
    Teaching young playwrights / Gerald Chapman ; edited and developed
by Lisa A. Barnett.
        p.   cm.
    Includes bibliographical references (p   ).
    ISBN 0-435-08212-4
    1. Drama—Study and teaching. I. Barnett, Lisa A. II. Title.
PN1701.C44   1990
    808.2—dc20   90-44760
                                                                        CIP

Designed by Maria Szmauz.
Cover photo by Chris Davies, London.
Printed on Demand 2000

Contents

1   Getting Started   1

2   Dramatic Action: Some Exercises   9

3   Teaching Empathy: The Key To Characterization   23

Exercises

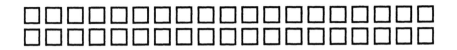

Notes on the Text

The manuscript Gerald Chapman left at his death was a complex survey of all that he had learned as a teacher of young playwrights. When I came to work for Heinemann in 1988, after working ten years for another drama publisher, I was offered the chance to go through what Gerald had left, and uncover the book he had written.

The book you have here is Gerald's book, a synthesis of his experience and knowledge. The voice you hear is his. In organizing and editing the text I tried to clarify a progression that was evident in the original. It meant rearranging the manuscript. It meant cutting out a lot of extraneous material that, while fascinating, interfered with the transmission of information. It meant some rewriting of explanatory passages. It meant structuring the exercises in a consistent manner. All of the information I needed to do this was there; it simply needed to be dug out and placed in its proper position.

Lisa A. Barnett

A Letter to Gerald Chapman from Dorothy Heathcote

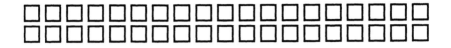

Dear Gerald,

I regret that you can now never read these words I write in sincere admiration of your book, which must stand as your memorial and the explanation to others of your teaching and creative obsessions.

I read the text with a dawning excitement as you guided me carefully and patiently through the maze of what a play consists of, and into the classrooms filled with humans, which the teacher in you needed so that the circle of yourself, the class members, and your craft could be completed.

Your book contains no glib generalizations. Instead, like an engineer, you patiently strip down that which we call a play into all its structural parts. *There* is the evidence that you gained mastery of your craft. You constantly remind me that you are a teacher—an enabler of others' knowing—as you introduce me to various people, warn me of and help me to share in the careful delicacy of your teaching: its attention to detail and its minute particularization in the management of words, space, time. I see you as a midwife, content to assist in the birthing of the creations of others, respectful, courteous, and attention-giving. Classes receive no bland praise or "blanket" comforts; rather they come under your cool, honoring eye, engaged without self-interest, allowing them to grow through their own abilities.

I am now, by my own will, retired from the active teaching that took me into classrooms, as your work did, to explore mutual

learning experiences with students and their teachers. If I were still
engaged thus, I would be saying something like this:

"Use this book by Gerald Chapman not as a treatise or a theo-
retical discourse. To do so is to miss the essence of his work and
the effort he made in his last months, weeks, days, to bring together
all his accumulated experience so that you may gain some of the
insights he won through practice. He does not ask you to copy his
ideas or his methods—only to patiently engage with him, visualizing
as you read those classes in action he presents, and hopefully his
work will invoke in you memories of other classes familiar to you
from your own practice.

"Slowly read and re-read his words which explain what a play
is, until they are a part of *your* understanding. When you see or
read a play for the pleasure of it, let Gerald's words occasionally
intrude to guide you to the interior structure of such works, and trust
yourself to introduce such experiences to your classes.

"Trust children as Gerald did; consider them colleagues, and
thank goodness that Gerald was able to 'get his act together' so that
you are the beneficiary."

These things I would say, Gerald. Thank you. This book shall
be your living, working (as the yeast works in bread) monument. You
need no tablets of stone.

In humility and friendship—

Dorothy

How To
Use This Book

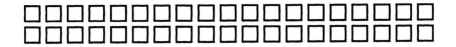

This book is based on playwriting workshops my colleagues and I conducted in New York City from 1981 onward. These workshops, involving students between the ages of nine and eighteen, usually took place in school and lasted a whole day, with a half-day follow-up a week or so later. An entire class of up to thirty-five students would be involved—a marathon experience, deliberately as intense a period of instruction as possible. Sometimes we would conduct shorter sessions, lasting perhaps two class periods, but we found that the novelty of playwriting required more time and a special involvement, so we tried to maintain the marathon format whenever possible.

This book is intended for both the experienced and inexperienced drama teacher. For the instructor who does not have the time or the inclination to read this book straight through, it may be used as a kind of recipe book. For teachers with little or no experience in teaching drama, this book offers an introduction to the simplest techniques of role-playing and improvisation, and defines their function in terms of teaching young playwrights. It is by no means a fully detailed description of creative dramatics (on which there are many excellent books already available, as noted in the bibliography). These are the basics of creative drama in the classroom, designed to use in the training of playwriting skills rather than acting skills.

I feel it is important for both teacher and student to get right into the act of playwriting; therefore, the first part of the book is almost completely practical. Chapters 1-5 contain exercises that both the inexperienced and experienced teacher need in order to get started right away. Chapters 6 and 7 take the lessons offered in the first five chapters and discuss them in terms of constructing a play, and evaluation and revision. Chapters 8-10 look at the theory behind the practice and offer some guidance in avoiding common errors and misconceptions—traps for the teacher that are easy to fall into, yet easily avoided.

Playwriting in the classroom involves several activities that can be grouped under four headings: Reading, both aloud and silently; Talking, in discussion as well as in improvisation or acting; Writing, individually and in groups; and Analyzing, as individuals or as a group. Try to bring all four elements into play from the earliest lesson onward. For example, if you can devote only one period a week for four weeks to playwriting, don't leave the actual writing until the last period. After briefly outlining your objectives, try one of the exercises such as the Headlines exercise (see Chapter 2), and follow it immediately with the Collaborative Writing Game (see Chapter 5). For a homework assignment, have the students read one or more of the plays suggested in the bibliography. Brief suggestions for lessons two through four might be as follows:

☐ Lesson Two. Discuss the homework reading, including clarification of the conventions of dramatic structure. Work through one of the improvisations suggested in Chapter 4. Homework: begin writing a draft of the improvisation, writing the scene preceding or immediately following the action of the improvisation.

☐ Lesson Three. Continue writing or revising scenes. Share some of the scenes in groups. Discuss what dramatic conventions were used. How did the scenes revise the improvised first draft? Homework: continue the play, or assign an observation/writing exercise.

☐ Lesson Four. Share the plays-in-progress and the observation exercises in small, separate, and simultaneous groups. Interpreting Text: Act out some of the observation exercises. Develop them, through improvisations and the Headlines exercise, into material for further playwriting.

These preliminary, sample lessons involve writing, improvisation, performance, practice in both dramatic conventions and dramatic layout, and introduction to the concepts of characterization and narrative structure.

Even covering half this material in the same amount of time would accomplish a lot. Or this material could be expanded to fill eight periods instead of four. There are many options, but each lesson should incorporate a minimum of points using a maximum of techniques. That is, to discuss each point of dramatic structure, use all possible means of exploring that point. *Each lesson* should include some writing, improvisation, and discussion. The first lesson should include the Collaborative Writing Game, as it is terrific and sometimes unexpected fun, and a good way of breaking the ice. It is a guaranteed technique for teaching structure as well as the ensemble spirit that theatre demands. The final lesson should involve a performance of some kind, however simple. Try not to be too ambitious too early—and always make sure a photocopier is available!

I hope that the contents guide you in planning your lessons. And I hope you have fun, as well as success, not only in your teaching, but in your own playwriting!

1

□□□□□□□□□□□□□□□□□□□□□□
□□□□□□□□□□□□□□□□□□□□□□

Getting Started

■■■■■■■■■■■■■■■■■■■■■■

Talking About Plays

On my first visit to a school in East Harlem, I was worried—would the children reject me because I was white, middle class, and, above all, foreign? I walked into the room wearing jeans and an open-necked shirt, and the teacher introduced me in a way that made it seem as if I were doing New York City itself, let alone the class, a huge favor: "This gentleman has come all the way from the Dramatists' Guild"— approximately sixty-six blocks—"I expect you to give him your undivided attention." Not an introduction to make the students trust you. A few narrowed their eyes and pursed their lips in a mask of critical apprehension, while others hunched over their desks or stared out the window. After the teacher left me alone with them, I asked the students to help me rearrange the room so we could all sit in a circle. I gave them a few seconds before I started to move the furniture. In those few seconds, they had time to realize that I was English and that I was not wearing a bowler hat or carrying an umbrella. The masks cracked. Giggles and chatter broke like a wave over the desks and chairs as we pushed them around. The workshop had begun.

This first minute of uproar can be very useful. Here it relaxed and invigorated the kids, promised them something unusual. It asserted my authority in a reasonable, non-threatening way, allowed the children to express their embarrassment safely, and gave me the chance to see how they behaved. I noticed who offered to help me directly, who was the loner, who sat next to whom, and who sat outside the circle until I invited her into it.

I announce the plan for the workshop: "We're here to learn how to write plays. We'll talk for a bit about plays, then you'll do some

1

acting—who likes acting here?—and then I'll ask you to write a scene for a play, which you can read out loud and which we'll talk about afterward. We'll have a lunch break around 11:30, OK?" The routine was broken—but the students are still here to learn. There will be variety, group and individual work, and a final product, which will be evaluated by the class as a group. A word of caution: Do not promise too much. If you have no facilities for a fully staged performance, or if the standard of work is not yet ready for a more public showing, then let the reading of the scripts among the group be a sufficient achievement.

If you are working with a new group of children, particularly if the children themselves are unknown to you, the way introductions are made can help command concentration and encourage the students to think about the topic in hand. I prefer to work with the kids in a circle around an empty space large enough to improvise in but small enough to create a feeling of intimacy, of being one group. There is an element of democracy in this arrangement, but the teacher is clearly the chairperson.

If, however, you are working with a group of students you know well, have worked with before, it is still worth going through the ritual of introductions around the circle. You and the students may well be surprised at how differently you see people you thought you knew well.

Introductions—Creating Dramatis Personae

If you're working with students whom you see every day, the ritual of introduction is still important and will be very useful, not only to the students, but to you, as you discover just how the students choose to present themselves when given this opportunity.

As the children introduce themselves around the circle, write their names on the blackboard. Ask them to say something about themselves, what they like doing, whether they have written plays, poems, or stories before, who their favorite people are. Introduce yourself in the same way—you are asking them to share information about themselves and must show that you are willing to do the same. The notes you make on the board beside each name demonstrate how seriously you accept what the students have chosen to say. This is important: the kids have selected to present themselves in a particular way, which you must accept. Even as I ask them questions about their interests, I encourage them to find out things about me. I ask them to guess where

I am from and to say what they know about England. I tell them what my job is and ask, "What does a theatre director do?"

As the children speak in turn, you will be able to assess their reaction to the situation you have created and find out what they think of "Why we are here." Tracy will say she has written a Nativity play. Susan will describe her short story about a horse. Herby will say nothing at all, except his name, and that so softly that you mishear it and misspell it on the blackboard. If you are working with a new group of students, always check that you have correctly spelled their names, as it is a part of their identity, the characters they see themselves as. You may find that more of the students have written in one form or another than you had realized or anticipated.

There are several drama games you can use to help introduce the students to one another. One is to have them clap their hands to a rhythm and then have each one say his or her name, followed by a favorite food. I prefer to let them characterize themselves in their own ways; I try to imagine them as dramatis personae. If Herby wants to be silent, I think of him as a silent and mysterious character in a play. I remember how Kristina said two of the things she liked doing were roller skating and watching babies. I begin to weave scenarios in my head. Encourage the kids to do the same, to regard each other as potential characters in an infinite variety of plays. You have to be careful, however, to avoid making them feel self-conscious or threatened. Keep the tone playful—this is only an exercise: "Suppose you were going to make up a play about some of the people in this class—which ones would you choose, and why?"

This will give you an insight into what peer structure is in place, and will either confirm or completely contradict what you have already noted on the board. For example, if someone chooses Tracy to be in his play because she is such a wild character, always getting into trouble, you can ask that person, "Then what kind of a Nativity play would Tracy have written?"

This exercise does two things. It begins to define character for the students as a combination of someone's self-perception and other people's perceptions. It also gives students status by casting them in roles in which they have a big investment. Encourage this casting of real people in make-believe plays by deliberately choosing some of the shyer—or even lazier or ruder—kids for your play. The silent Herby, for example, could be the mysterious stranger in town. You will have to be careful not to let this exercise become psychodrama—avoid saying "I would choose Herby as a shy kid who gets beaten by his parents," as this could conceivably be too close to the truth. Create a distance between the real person and the fictional character in order to protect the child's privacy. You can also do this by changing a character's name.

Tracy could become José. José is rebelling against his parents. Why does he rebel? Would José write a Nativity play as part of his rebellion, or as a way of pleasing his parents? You retain the interesting elements that have been offered for this character, but you release the class from the need to stick to literal truth.

Creating dramatis personae out of the students' introductions must involve, therefore, a distancing device. You can build complexity into this exercise by asking the students for as many different imaginary variations on the reasons for someone's behavior as possible. Why does wild Tracy/José write a Nativity play? Because

☐ She wants to surprise her parents, and make up with them, or . . .
☐ She wants to play the part of the Innkeeper, or . . .
☐ She hates the traditional Nativity play and wants to write a New Wave version to shock her parents, or . . .

In each case, the rebel instincts are somehow connected to Tracy's own desire to write a Nativity play, but her point of view changes depending on the scenario. By soliciting such examples of character traits in action, you teach the students that a single trait can have a multitude of meanings. Take Herby's silence, for example. There are many famous dramatic examples of a silent character and what that silence means . . . and what happens as a result:

☐ Thomas More, in *A Man For All Seasons*, is silent because he does not wish to incriminate himself; but others choose to view his silence as incriminating, and it costs him his life.
☐ Cordelia is silent because she loves her father, King Lear, too much to flatter him. Her silence costs her his love, and she is banished.
☐ Mother Courage refuses to acknowledge the dead body of her son for fear of endangering herself and the rest of her family. Her silence is at war with her maternal feelings.

Ask the students for their own examples of silence in action, and compare them with examples from dramatic literature. In this way, the students start to view their own work as part of an artistic tradition, and this helps give status to their work.

This discussion can lead to a writing exercise based on some of their suggestions. You will have to give them some guidance, because the danger is that silence simply leads to impasse. Examples:

☐ A freedom fighter refuses to admit to his captors some vital information.
☐ The school principal demands to know who broke the windows in the gym. No one owns up.
☐ A girl asks her boyfriend if he likes her new hairstyle. He says nothing.

Each scene will remain dead if the insistent questioning is met with silence. A change has to occur. Silence must cost a character something. This can be the first lesson in what the word *dramatic* actually means: drama is not the conflict itself, but the changes arising from the conflict. The freedom fighter might admit the information, the principal could close the gym as punishment, and the boy might use the chance to dump his girlfriend. In each case, the breaking of the impasse leads to a new situation. Ask the students what happens next, and let them write their own versions of the next scene, reminding them that their main character must face some sort of choice and change as a result, and that any change must build on whatever has happened previously in the play.

A supplemental exercise would be to ask the kids to dramatize the silence from the point of view of someone who is not the actual protagonist—of someone who might be affected by another person's silence. An interesting problem—how do you dramatize an offstage silence? In the case of the prisoner, the scene could be set in a cell next to where he is being interrogated. If the other prisoners are also freedom fighters, their colleague's silence is precious to them. This technique of sharpening our focus by looking at something obliquely will encourage the kids to think and write creatively, rather than just literally.

Herby's silence, therefore, becomes the springboard for a lively and imaginative introduction into characterization and the basis for several writing exercises! But you must always honor his privacy and make it clear to all your students that the job of the playwright is to treat real life as fiction.

These exercises teach the children to be more specific in their character descriptions, and to view characters—even "villains"—from more than one angle. It suggests to them that they can achieve this best by trying to go beyond the literal truth and search for the imaginative truth. Children have a natural facility for shifting back and forth from reality to fiction. The teacher's task is to help develop this ability into a craft that will harness and direct their imagination, and turn their playwriting into something more than mere reporting.

Exercise

□□□□□□□□□□□□□□□□□□□□□□□□□□□□□□□□

Life Histories

The playwright Edward Bond used this exercise with a group of teen-agers in a workshop at the Royal Court Theatre, London.

Strike a match, and describe your life history while the match remains alight between your fingers.

There are two objectives to be achieved with this brief exercise: first, it introduces the students to the concept of storytelling as the basis for playwriting, and second, it introduces them to the need for careful selection of material. It also imposes several disciplines on the young participants: the time limit, the skill in keeping the match alight, the awesome task of selecting the data they want to present. The guttering flame is as final as the curtain at the end of a play. It enforces economy of expression, and it gives them an action on which everything depends. It makes them, in effect, the actors of their own life histories. By the time the last teenager did this exercise at the Royal Court, the lesson had been learned. He lit the match, paused, said two words—and blew the match out. The actor had turned dramatist.

A variation of this exercise (one that is less risky than playing with fire) is to ask the students to make paper airplanes, and to describe their lives, or their greatest ambitions, while the plane is in flight. The very act of making the airplane teaches an important dramatic lesson. Unlike a match, which is premade and can be easily controlled, a paper plane has to be expertly crafted beforehand if it is to fly at all. A technical flaw will bring down even the most poetic of ambitions. I remember launching my airplane and saying, "I should like to be a conductor. . . ." even as my plane nose-dived into the floor!

What Makes Good Plays?
Developing A Shared Language

Find out if the students have already written plays, acted in them, or even seen them. If the answer to all these questions is no, then ask what movies they have seen. Encourage their enthusiasm. Find out what their favorite parts were, what they liked, what they found boring or difficult to understand. From this discussion, move onto the questions: "What do you think are the most important things to have in a

good play? Why?" The answers will form the basis for the entire discussion and for all your teaching of these young playwrights, because
from these answers, you and they will develop a common language,
a shared understanding of what you all hope to achieve. Among the
values listed by a group of sixth graders I worked with were:

☐ Plays must be acted well. [Everyone's a critic!]
☐ Plays are visual—not just words.
☐ Plays must be real.
☐ The meaning must be clear.
☐ Plays should not be racist—they must be honest about people.
☐ A play must grab the audience's attention, so they can relate to
   and be involved with it.
☐ Lots of action. This is how the meaning is conveyed.
☐ Everyone has to cooperate in order to put the play on.

This is a start. Using the list makes it easier to illustrate the strengths
and weaknesses of their points with regard to dramatic structure. Certainly a play must be visual—the words must be used to paint the
pictures, to create the emotional resonances the young playwright is
after. That plays must be real is an interesting point—these students
had realized that reality is not limited to everyday life, but that the
playwright has a responsibility to make everything he or she proposes
real, before the audience can suspend its disbelief. Virtually all the
points parallel or paraphrase more conventional principles of good
playwriting. The students are on the right track.

These comments include the students' own words and my own
paraphrasing. They remained on the board throughout the workshop
as a reference to the principles we wanted to hold to; it helped turn
the students into a critical audience. What the teacher then has to do
is analyze what the students mean by whatever values they propose,
and weld them into a shared concept of what makes a good play.

Let us consider the basic elements of theatre and playmaking, using
as reference the points raised by these sixth graders.

2

Dramatic Action:
Some Exercises

"Lots of action" is what children often mean when they say "plays should be interesting" or "plays should be dramatic." At PS 346, the discussion centered on the sixth graders' feeling that "a play must grab the audience's interest so that the audience can relate to and be involved with it." I want to analyze these points in reverse order, showing how audience involvement depends on understanding exactly what dramatic action is.

Characters exist in specific situations, and behave accordingly. They act and react—realistically—to the situations in which they find themselves. Character is where dramatic action develops.

Children who are weaned on television drama, with its car chases and nonstop, often cartoon, violence, often think that dramatic action is synonymous with exciting incidents. People falling off cliffs, gun battles, or close encounters with objects or beings in outer space are all thought of as being "dramatic," but they are all so short-lived and insubstantial that it takes a constant, quick succession of them to maintain our interest. Life is rarely a succession of such incidents; if it were, it would be unbearable. Rather, events such as these mark climaxes or turning points in otherwise ordinary lives.

Exercise

□ □

Headlines—Finding the Drama Behind the Dramatic Moment.

Objective: To help students discern the true drama behind a "dramatic" moment. *Moment* is a key word to remember. It is over in an instant. What lies *behind* that moment is the true drama. This realization helps students avoid piling incident upon incident in their plays in the interest of "lots of action."

Discuss headlines, how they catch our eye, and how, the more sensationalistic they are, the less inclined we are to take them seriously. Examples:

BURIED ALIVE! A LIVING DEATH!
MAN CUTS OFF OWN HEAD WITH CHAIN SAW—AND LIVES!
SPACE INVADERS LAND ON VILLAGE GREEN!

Some are just too sensational to do much with. A level of headlines, usually from the daily papers, is just slightly above these, and shows more potential:

UNIDENTIFIED BODY FOUND IN EAST RIVER!
HE SANG—HE DIED!

We turn the pages and sigh, or giggle, or feel momentarily revolted before turning to the funnies or the sports pages or the crossword. Ask the class, What would make you pause before turning the page? What would make you stop in your tracks and avidly read every detail of the story that lies behind a headline? Someone may suggest, "If you knew the people in the story, or if you recognized something in the photograph."

One of the simplest and most effective ways of exploring background of the dramatic moment in search of the drama is to think in terms of motive. Suggest a hypothesis: "Suppose the body in the East River were wearing a bright red jacket with a Scorpio sign embroidered on the back—and you knew someone at school who wore a jacket just like that." Your interest would be aroused. What information would you expect the paper to reveal? What questions have been raised in your mind? How did this person die? Was it accident, suicide, or murder? You might get the following:

A shy boy named Jack. Drowned, apparently no sign of a struggle. Suicide? This, in turn, raises a further question. If suicide, why did Jack kill himself? Each response leads to a new question, drawing you further back in the story. Now, was Jack a shy boy? Such jackets are usually the province of the popular kids—or gang members. Was his shyness an act? What did it cover up? Why did someone as connected as he was commit suicide?

It would be easy to develop a lurid tale of drug dealing, frustrated teen love, remorse, and suicide—and who can say that just because it's lurid, it isn't true drama that occurs more often than we like to think? It is the sensationalistic we are trying to steer clear of—not the truth.

☐ Question One: Why did Jack commit suicide?
☐ Answer: Because he was depressed.
☐ Question Two: Why was he depressed?

It is at this point that questions can really lead to multiple answers, from which you can pick and choose, always following each answer to another question. Jack was depressed because . . .

Urge the students to keep it simple. Because he had one last, huge fight with his parents. Because he had had a fight with his girlfriend, and she said she would not see him anymore.

Question: Why did he fight with his parents or girlfriend? Why doesn't she want to see him anymore?

Answer: Because his parents did not want him to see certain of his friends anymore/Because his girlfriend hated the crowd Jack was running with.

Why?

Answer: More tangents, more possible directions. As the discussion develops, the students will offer more and more alternative answers to each Why. Encourage each student to note down his or her own version of the story.

This exercise demonstrates how we may enhance our interest in an incident by getting to know the people involved. This anticipates the next stage of the discussion—how an audience gets to know a character. If we know something about those involved, our curiosity will demand to be fed. This thinking process begins to parallel the dramatic process. The dramatist is not content merely to report or reenact an event. He gives an event significance by showing how and why it happened. Each event in a play must exist to answer a question. By systematically asking and answering the question *why*, the dramatist works out a structured narrative.

You can help the students structure their plot about Jack by suggesting that each *why* and its specific answer are individual scenes.

Suppose we call the scene wherein the body is discovered Scene X. The question is, Why did Jack commit suicide? This, then, is answered in the *previous* scene, Scene W: Jack is depressed. Why? Jack had a fight with his parents or girlfriend: Scene V. And so on. Ask the students for ideas on how to dramatize each of the different possibilities, but make sure each version of the scene really does answer the pertinent question—and addresses the relevant answer. Obviously, it is not good drama for Jack to state baldly that he is depressed and thinks he might kill himself. The problem in Scene W is to show Jack's state of mind. Jack himself might not even appear. His girlfriend may have remarked on his changed attitude; his parents might be worried about his moodiness. We will see that Jack is depressed. Scene V, the reason for Jack's depression, his fight with his girlfriend or parents, his wondering if his friends are really good friends, is more external, easier to dramatize.

A variation of this exercise could be to give your students the concluding situation of a famous play without telling them what the play is, and have them apply this questioning technique to work out the plot—see what comes up!

Employing a straightforward question-and-answer technique can begin very simply and develop into something rich and strange, depending on the time you have. With practice, the kids can do the exercise themselves: divide the class into groups and give each one a headline (or even the same one), and tell them to develop the drama behind this dramatic incident by telling the story in a logical sequence. Try the same exercise, but this time, move forward chronologically: What happens next, and why? This exercise makes explicit many of the basic principles of playwriting.

The inspiration for a play (in this case, Scene X) need not be the first scene of the play. A common error, even with mature writers, is to give the game away by putting what should be the climax of the drama right at the beginning. Build suspense by delaying the climax.

You can also build suspense by foreshadowing. The violence of Jack's argument with his parents, or with his girlfriend, could foreshadow his violent death.

Encourage the students to think of scene writing not as exposition, but as a part of a whole, and a way of manipulating the sequence of events—by inventing a cause, you also create an effect. Any play about Jack must make sense of his suicide; every scene leading up to the climax, therefore, must effectively close off more and more of Jack's options until it seems to him there is no other way out. Each scene provokes a change, however subtle. The effect is not random; it propels the story toward the denouement. Each scene fulfills a function, fitting into a pattern of questions and answers.

Tension can be increased by complicating the situation, increasing the pressure on the protagonist. A favorite example of mine is this:

You and a friend discover someone bleeding to death from a gunshot wound. You have to inform the authorities. But there is a power failure, and the lights do not work. The phone is at the end of a long, dark hallway, and the murderer could still be present.

If it were easy to call the police or the ambulance, the scene would be less dramatic. The necessary action loses its sense of danger, and its significance is minimized. An action, then, is dramatic not only because it reveals cause and effect, but because it imposes a choice on the characters. The conflict may never be resolved, but a choice must be made. The more difficult the choice, the greater the cost to the character. Jack refuses to break off with his circle of friends and stands to lose his girlfriend, or he refuses to go along with something his friends have planned—and could very well find himself in physical danger.

Point of View

By noting the different possible directions and ideas for each scene, you encourage the students to adopt a point of view. This is very natural—anyone who has ever related a story has done so from a particular viewpoint. It is important, however, for students to learn that a playwright must choose his point of view very carefully, for it will help determine the emotional tone of the work. If the writer wishes to focus on the problems of Jack's family, she might well dramatize the points of view of neighbors and friends—people outside what the writer is actually focusing on. If she wants to concentrate on Jack's growing isolation, the scenes could be written from the point of view of the gang or the rejected girlfriend.

This whole exercise emphasizes the value of craft. Situations are created and shaped in order to serve the playwright's purpose. It is a little like working as a detective except that, in this case, the playwright plants the clues—will this or that clue help or hinder the progress of the story? Would an alternative point of view create an illuminating contrast? What would increase the tension in a certain scene? It is vital for the playwright to know how to create the effects desired. Repeat this exercise as often as you wish: use headlines; photos without captions; existing poems, stories, or fables. Choose a point of departure, then begin the process of asking *why*. Build up the various scenarios into treatments for complete plays, always encouraging students to widen their focus by imagining as many different points of view as possible before they narrow it back down to their final choice. Split them into different writing groups, all with the same basic point being dramatized, and see how different viewpoints are being treated. What you are doing here is training the students to use their imagination as a laboratory in which human behavior is tested in an increasingly wider variety of situations. The scenewriting should spring from lively and imaginative discussions and improvisations (which will be discussed in chapter 4). The more practiced the students become at experiencing the dramatic possibilities of a situation, the easier it will be for them to improve their playwriting abilities. There will come a time when their scenes will develop from being rather sketchy, one-dimensional answers to a particular *why* to more complex scenes that contain multiple answers to several questions, and that may also simultaneously contrast several points of view. You can prepare for such a step by slowly building complexity into the discussion, as in the Headlines exercise, and by rewriting improvised scenes (see chapter 7). By approaching the matter of dramatic action in this way, you help the students steer clear of mere self-expression and guide them into a form of problem solving, which can be, and is, employed outside of playwriting. If we have to talk to the boss about a raise, we plan in advance the right moment and the right words. If we find out that a friend has betrayed us, we carefully choose the words and occasion to confront him. Dramatization requires no less imaginative preparation and precision. Once students understand this connection between life and art, they will understand more readily the importance of craft and technique, not just as formal disciplines, but as enjoyable means of solving imaginary (but no less real) social problems.

Narrators Never Tell the Whole Truth

Problem: In stories and novels, the writer can easily indicate what a character is thinking or feeling. In plays, these things have to be dramatized—shown—in action and in dialogue. We'll discuss this more fully in chapter 3, but we've already learned that one effective way of revealing and heightening a person's predicament is by using contrasting points of view to look at it.

One of the most common mistakes young playwrights make is to write a play as if it were a story with all the description left out. After a few minutes of dialogue, they find they need some description to advance the plot, and so they resort to using a narrator. This is usually unnecessary and unsuccessful. It is also usually untheatrical. (I say usually because I am aware of how the greatest dramatists, from the

Greeks to Arthur Miller, have occasionally used narrators.) If you use the *why* exercise and train the class always to find the proper moment and words to solve a problem, you should find that the narrator syndrome will quickly die out.

But there is a more problematic use of the narrator that is not so easy to tackle. It crops up frequently in adolescents' scripts as a kind of psychodramatic device, and in it, the narrator represents the sole point of view of the play. He is a character with privileged knowledge, either because it is actually the adolescent writer in disguise, or because it is a very strong projection of the writer's fantasies and wish-fulfillment. Even if the young writer has changed his name to a fictitious one, the play may remain so completely trapped by the immediate and subjective experiences of the author that its focus becomes too narrow. For example, if the play about Jack were written simply from his point of view, the funeral scene would have to be narrated by Jack's ghost— which has been done, with varying degrees of success! There are dangers to such an approach, however, because the tendency will be to diminish the humanity of the other characters in favor of the egocentric universe of the narrator.

This problem applies to young writers who wish to focus on something very personal. They choose a main character to represent this personal viewpoint, but they will tend to see things as happening to them all the time—acted upon, or reacting, rather than acting. Consequently, the protagonist becomes extremely passive, an observer rather than a doer. Hero as victim simply does not work. In Edmund Tyrone (*Long Day's Journey Into Night*), Eugene O'Neill masterfully created a version of this kind of character, and he did it deliberately, making it fulfill a dramatic purpose. A symptom of this narrator/protagonist syndrome is the use of a narrator who reports everything secondhand. The protagonist/author is removed from the action and remains, God-like, above it all. For example, Andrea Dunbar (a member of one of our British workshops), fifteen years old when she wrote *The Arbor*, wrote the first draft of one of the play's central scenes as reported speech, an extended stage-direction, really. The scene concerned a fight over a soccer ball between her brother and the next-door neighbor's boy:

Late one evening, a boy called Peter was playing football outside on the field.
He wanted to fight an Irish boy who had kicked him and run away.
So Peter went over to the house and shouted for him to come out.
He wouldn't.
The woman who lived there came out and said she'd fight Peter but he wouldn't.
Peter's dad came up to see what the trouble was about.

The girl who had just come back from baby-sitting at Joan's went over to her brother, who was standing with Peter, to get her mother's cigarettes.

The woman chased her and the girl's brother shouted at the woman, who picked up a brick and threw it at Peter's dad's wagon.

He moved it out of the way because his two young children were in it and backed it into a lamp post. So he said he was going to ring the police.

The police came in about five minutes by which time Peter, the girl's brother, and the girl had moved to the other side of the field.

The police went over to see what the trouble was and they were told but they told them to ignore the woman and go home.

But nobody moved.

The girl's brother was swearing and saying why should they.

But they finally went and stood outside their own house and talked to the girl's mother.

The Police went so they all went down to the bottom of the street to talk to a neighbor. She went in, after a while, the Irish boy came out again and so did another boy called Tony.

They all started shouting and several police cars came back and stopped at the bottom of the street.

It was very funny to read, but it was not yet a play. We asked Andrea why she had not written the dialogue. "Well, I weren't there; I watched it through window," was her reply. "Why don't you use your imagination?" we asked. "Oh, can you do that in a play?" she said, and went away and rewrote it and turned it into something wonderful:

WIFE: Right you lot. I'm just sick of you now. Who wants to fight me? Come on! Come on! (Nobody moves) What's wrong with you? All frightened of a woman are you?

CHRIS: Oh get in you silly bag. We're not cowards. We don't hit women.

(She runs and grabs Christopher and starts hitting him. Somebody goes and tells his mum and she comes out followed by her husband)

CHRIS's MUM: Look you Irish bastard what do you think you've been playing at?

MARTIN's WIFE: I've hit him for giving me a load of old buck. He deserves it anyway, because he's nothing but a cheeky little sod.

CHRIS's MUM: Are you trying to say I should belt my kids?

MARTIN's WIFE: I am, yes.

CHRIS's MUM: And what fucking right have you got to tell me that?

MARTIN's WIFE: I've got every right, seeing as how he's been cheeky to me.

CHRIS's MUM: Oh, so you're saying yours are not then?

MARTIN's WIFE: Yes. Mine aren't cheeky to people.

CHRIS's MUM: Fucking hell! Have you heard her? Let me tell you something. Yours are the cheekiest lot of bastards going.

MARTIN's WIFE: Don't you call my kids bastards!

CHRIS's MUM: Why? What are you going to do about it?

MARTIN'S WIFE: Well let's look at it this way, yours are a bigger set of bastards.

CHRIS'S DAD: Don't you ever let me hear you call my kids bastards again.

MARTIN: Take your dirty hands off my wife.

CHRIS'S DAD: I won't. Not until she says she's sorry for what she's done.

MARTIN: You'd better fucking do or I'll flatten you, you bald-headed bastard. You're nowt else!

(A police car comes patrolling round and stops)

POLICE: What's going on here?

CHRIS'S DAD: It's this Irish bastard here, calling my kids bastards.

MARTIN: Well you called my kids bastards.

CHRIS'S DAD: Oh fuck off will you!

POLICE: There's no need for the swearing.

CHRIS'S DAD: Look, rubber-lips. You don't know what's been going on here, so it would just be better for you to go and find some of these murderers instead of coming here over some neighborhood argument.

POLICE: Look here you. Don't tell me what to do unless you want to end up in the cells.

(There is a crowd of people watching)

Come on everybody. Let's have you home. Come on, move. You and all Dunbar.

DAVID: I won't.

POLICE: You will, sonny-boy, or I'll move you.

DAVID: You're not big enough yet, rubber-lips.

POLICE: You're a cheeky bastard young Dunbar.

DAVID: Well I can't say much for you, rubber-lips. You're a load of shit. *(To the other boys)* Isn't he lads?

LADS: Yes, that's right.

PETER: Go on, give it to him Dave.

POLICE: If you're not gone from here in sixty seconds I'll run the bastard lot of you in.

DAVID: It's gonna take a lot more than you rubber-lips. I'll bring me dad over in a minute and he'll knock you off your bleedin' feet.

POLICE: Oh yes. Go and get him then.

DAVID: I won't. I don't need him anyway. I can do it myself. You're a load of crap rubber-lips!

(Everybody laughs)

POLICE: Look here son, are you gonna move? I'll give you one more chance.

DAVID: Don't you call me son!

POLICE: Right, that's it! Stop where you are, I'll soon have you moved.

POLICE: *(To Policeman Rubber-lips)* What's wrong then?

RUBBER-LIPS: It's young Dunbar here refusing to move.

POLICE: Okay then, we'll run him in. How old is this youth?

DAVID: Eighteen. Why?

POLICE: Right, you're under arrest.

GIRL: He's not. He's only seventeen—let go of him, you bastards. Go tell my mum somebody. Hurry up.

DAVID: Don't fucking pull me about. What do you think I am? A bastard rag doll?

POLICE: Shut your mouth. Or I'll stick my boot in it.

DAVID: Go on then if you think you're so fucking hard don't say it, fucking do it! Yes. You're all mouth and no action you set of bastards!

POLICE: Being cheeky like that's not gonna get you anywhere. Nor is that language you're using.

DAVID: Well you lot fucking use it don't you?

GIRL: (*Grabbing David's coat*) Let him go you bastards, don't take him! Let him go! (*Putting him in the car*)

(*The Girl's mother comes out followed by her sister and her father who is running down the street pulling his trousers up*)

FATHER: Why have you got my son in that car? I want to know why you've got him in there.

RUBBER-LIPS: For obstructing the police.

FATHER: Obstructing my arse. I might have known you'd have something to do with it, rubber-lips.

MOTHER: What's wrong, Brian?

FATHER: You'd better ask them.

GIRL: They've arrested our David.

MOTHER: What for?

GIRL: 'Cause he wouldn't move.

MOTHER: What are they doing with him?

GIRL: Taking him to the police station.

MARTIN: Up the IRA!!

CHRIS'S DAD: Get in you Irish bastard.

MARTIN: You an' all you English bastard.

CHRIS'S DAD: Oye, screws—go and take him instead of picking on kids.

RUBBER-LIPS: Go home.

CHRIS'S DAD: I won't.

MARTIN: Up the IRA!

GIRL: Let him go!

2ND POLICEMAN: Go home. (*Grabbing her*)

GIRL: I won't. And you can take your dirty fucking hands off me.

MARTIN: Up the IRA!

MOTHER: Oh will you shut up.

GIRL: Here mum, throw this brick at them.

2ND POLICEMAN: Put that brick down.

This leap from accurate but passive observation to active engagement in a situation by stepping into someone else's shoes is the key to dramatizing an experience, and it forces the imagination to work more creatively. Andrea's second draft was "truer" than the first even though she invented the dialogue. It was truer because it allowed us to judge the street fight from more than one vantage point. By fictionalizing this scene, Andrea was able to present it more objectively. Take the familiar and make sense of it with what is unfamiliar.

Presenting the Evidence: The Importance of Being Specific

Andrea moved from observing an event as an outsider to imagining in great detail what it was like to be in the thick of it. Some young writers actually move in the other direction, from an actual experience to a watered-down reporting of it. Frequently, the reason for this is defensive—to protect privacy or to avoid reliving the pain of the original experience. This is what a thirteen-year-old girl from a school in Harlem wrote during a workshop:

(Wendy was walking home after the party. It was late. Her mother had warned her not to go out so late)

MAN: *(From dark)* Come here!

WENDY: Help!

(The man ran away. Wendy was dirty and sick. She felt blood sticking to her legs. When she got home, she couldn't tell her mother)

The only moment that is dramatized is the assault on Wendy, but this barely lasts longer than a second. Everything else has to be assumed or narrated. The author had intended to communicate something intensely felt, but she had not succeeded. In helping this writer, we had to be careful not to make her feel even more vulnerable. Simply asking her to write her play with more factual detail would be cruel, could only frighten her. The important thing is to show how an audience can feel sympathy for Wendy by sharing in her feelings. This means we should see her in all the situations that lead up to the assault so that we can understand her state of mind. It is also clear that the crisis of the assault precipitates an even bigger crisis of being unable to face her mother. We will understand this fully, though, only if we know in advance what the mother is like. The suggestion to the author was that the biggest drama is actually the confrontation scene at home, and that the assault scene (which suggests rape but deliberately side-steps it) does not have to be staged in great detail. This releases the author from the potential humiliation and embarrassment that the writer might feel if asked to fill in the details of the story. If the writer can understand that the real climax of the story is the audience's feeling sorry for Wendy at the very moment her mother is scolding her for disobedience, it will be easier to suggest a dramatic structure that will lead to such a climax:

SCENE T: Mother tells Wendy not to go out late.
SCENE U: Wendy at the party, happy and oblivious of the time.
SCENE V: Wendy leaving the party, unable to get a ride home.
SCENE W: The assault.
SCENE X: Wendy at home. She cleans herself up secretly, but is interrupted by her angry mother.

It is not even necessary to dramatize the assault. Dramatic literature is full of "unwritten scenes," one of the most famous being the rape in *A Streetcar Named Desire*. Neither does Scene X have to be the last scene of the play. Wendy has an urgent need to exorcise her feelings of pain and disgust. In Scene X, the audience sees Wendy make a choice—to remain silent—but this does not resolve her problem. The author can take the play further on its journey and show how this added tension will change Wendy's behavior, how much it will cost her, and how this will, in turn, change her character as it is perceived by the audience.

Here is a different example of the same problem, except that this time the young author was dealing with a fantasy instead of a nightmare. After a few lines of dialogue, the narrator came in:

Angel and Suneeta held hands, sitting on the beach by the fire, and watched the sunset. They stayed there until dawn the next day.

Then the dialogue picked up again, and it was the same type of inconsequential stuff we had had earlier:

— How are you?
— OK. And you?
— OK, thanks. Shall we go home?
— OK.

We missed the drama because it had been tucked inside the narration/stage direction. Those two sentences are impossible to stage on their own. The imagination would have to flesh them out. What did they talk about? Did they only hold hands or did they make love? Was it an enjoyable experience for both of them? Does their stiff, bloodless little exchange the following morning give any indication of how they feel about what happened or did not happen? None of this is clarified. We are simply given a teenage fantasy, as pathetic and yearning in its implications as any found inside a romance magazine. But it is locked inside the writer's head, from whence it was transferred to the page without having gone through the imaginative process of sifting, clarifying, and selecting the means of expressing it. Because the theatre is a live medium, what actually happens on stage has to be very specific. The particularities of dialogue and action have to be rigorously supplied. There is no other way an audience can see into a character's mind and know what a character is thinking and feeling, let alone what the author is fantasizing. In this respect, playwriting may force a student to use his imagination more demandingly than does short-story writing; it certainly imposes a stringent imaginative discipline.

The final thing that a teacher should reiterate when dealing with dramatic action or its substitute, the narrator, is that plays are located within specific places, at specific times, and deal with specific actions. This journey has a timetable and a road map! Have your students ask themselves:

☐ *What* is happening?
☐ *Where* is this happening?
☐ *When* is it happening?

And then, for every action that occurs—*why*. Armed with precise answers to these elementary questions, the young playwright will be able to deal with the more complex question of characterization.

3

□□□□□□□□□□□□□□□□□□□□
□□□□□□□□□□□□□□□□□□□□

Teaching Empathy: The Key To Characterization

■■■■■■■■■■■■■■■■■■■■■

In order for an audience to relate to and be involved in a play, it must be involved in the characters as well as the action, since character creates action and action refines character. Plot has been defined as character in action.

Many teachers make the mistake of teaching dramatic characterization by first asking students to write soliloquies, or monologues. For two reasons, I believe this is a mistake. First, monologues are very difficult to write for theatre; they do not easily fit into a dramatic context and therefore require a sophistication and experience that the apprentice playwright simply does not yet possess. Second, monologues present only one side of a character. Moreover, it is the one side of a person that, not surprisingly, we do not often see, the private person, the part that a character, deliberately or not, hides from everyone else. This does not mean that what we are seeing or hearing in a monologue is the very essence of a character, or that it is more truthful than the masks assumed in public. It is actually harder to develop believable, human characters in the vacuum of a monologue than in the crucible of conflict with other characters and with events. Writing monologues should not be the first step toward empathizing with a character. Encourage the class to think of characters as being active in social relationships before thinking of them as passive in contemplation.

Ask the students, How do you get to know someone—the new pupil at school, or the next-door neighbors? You watch them, you test them, to see how they respond, how they behave, what governs their actions, what they say. All these things may or may not confirm first impressions, but they offer a more just view of that person. The first rule about characterization is, be fair. Give the characters a chance in life by spending time with them. The single biggest flaw in young people's playwriting is underwriting, making scenes so short and action so spare that we have no time to get to know the characters involved and therefore no time to judge them. Your advice to your playwrights should be: Make friends with your characters by spending time with them, in all different situations, so that you and the audience learn about their tastes, their lifestyles, their beliefs. Ask the students for examples of how they got to know the personalities of their best friends or their worst enemies. In either case, the process was probably the same.

"Making friends" is a metaphor for the process. It does not mean you have to agree with, let alone have any great affection for, your character. Unless you are passionately interested in him or her, how can you expect to engage the audience's interest?

Here are some approaches to the question, How do we get to know someone?

Exercise

☐ ☐

Playground Fight

Creating Character From Context

There has been a fight in the playground, and the two participants plus a witness are giving their separate accounts of it to the principal. The class is to act as a kind of jury, taking notes on what people say, while you as teacher, in the role of the principal, also make notes on the blackboard.

The three volunteers you choose from the class to improvise this scene should not have any time to consult with each other. The directions for this improvisation are that whatever one person says, the other should disagree with (see chapter 4 for other examples of Conflict Improvs), and offer a different version. The witness is free to agree or disagree with either version, or even to make up a third one. After they have each given their account, ask the jury for its opinions on who is telling the truth. Encourage the three volunteers to remain in character in order to answer questions from the class. Then, tell the students that they, too, were witnesses, and invite them to write a scene depicting their account of the events leading up to the fight, concentrating on the three characters already presented.

That is one possibility. A variation would be to divide the class into groups of four (the two fighters, the witness, and the neutral observer/notetaker), and ask them to improvise in different parts of the room. Emphasize that no one disputes that a fight took place; the dispute is over why it happened and who started it. Written scenes and improvisations should stop before the first blow is made—this helps control the tendency to focus on the "drama" of the fight. The scene can even take place much earlier than when the fight starts—perhaps the conflict that led to the fight occurred a day or even a week before. Don't limit the students—just find out from each group why this fight took place.

The most crucial part of this exercise is the reading out or showing of the individual scenes. Why? It is here we see the development of the different characters in the students' treatments. It is also here we take the first steps toward revision and rewriting. We also see the reasons different students chose to believe different accounts and how they dramatized their reasons. The class may have trusted one protagonist over the other because she is the class leader or favorite. Such trust could be subverted by a *post-fight* scene that reveals how this leader connives to protect her position by manipulating events.

As you listen to or observe each scene, it is worth spending quite a lot of time pointing out how partial one's view of any event is, how the two scenes (the scene before the fight and the one in the office) both dramatize actual events but in contradictory ways. Select an example from the students' scenes, have it read aloud, and then follow it with a reenactment of the office scene. You will find that the office scene will now begin to be rewritten, adapted by the performers to sharpen the points of contradiction. For example, if one fight scene has been written in a way that totally vindicates one of the protagonists, it is likely that that particular character will protest his innocence more forcefully now. We know he is innocent, but can the principal be sure? Now you, as the principal, should play devil's advocate. Instead of appealing for witnesses, you should insist that this character is always getting into trouble and going on about how innocent he is. You simply do not believe him! Give the other two characters in the scene a chance to own up and prevent a miscarriage of justice. If they do, continue the scene. If they do not, then stop the scene.

If the scene does continue with the confession, the principal and observing students will be forced to reconsider that what is now clear is only a partial view of the pupil's character. The pupil is no longer a deceitful manipulator; he has some truth in him, too! This complexity did not exist in the first draft of the office scene, yet it was set up in a moment, achieved by deliberately setting up a contrast between the audience's viewpoint (what they have seen and know to be true) and the principal's viewpoint (based on past events that we have to take as given). This ironic contrast is pushed toward a crisis when the principal's viewpoint is challenged by the other two pupils' viewpoint (based on an event, the truth of which the audience has witnessed).

On the other hand, if the scene stops at the imminent punishment of the innocent student because the other two pupils do not intervene, the complexity of characterization is heightened further. The audience's sense of justice will be outraged. Its identification with the innocent student will be enhanced by the student's isolation. And the demeanor of the other two is important in characterizing them: if they leave the office in shock, then a burden has been put on them that may anticipate a future scene in which they have to confront their victim. If they leave the office self-satisfied and grinning, the burden remains squarely on the victim's shoulders. We realize that the boy is a scapegoat.

This exercise teaches that character is not a trait, fixed at birth and forever immutable. It is relative, it changes not only according to situation but also according to other people's (including the audience's) attitudes and points of view. What appear to be genuine tears in a scene become crocodile tears when juxtaposed with another scene.

Discussion should focus on what later scenes could involve; how the innocent student reacts, what options are open to all the main characters. Follow the discussion with a written assignment: the next scene of the play. Observe how many students change the character of the innocent victim into a cool aggressor who may turn the tables on his peers, or even on the principal!

Character as Part of an Argument

Character is part of a continuous argument in a play—between the people on stage, the character, and the audience. Character is defined by the cut and thrust of different points of view, which is why performances of the same play evoke different responses. I will never forget one performance of a play called *Reggae Brittania* at the Royal Court Theatre. One of the characters was a school janitor who objected to the school auditorium being used for a reggae concert because it upset his routine—and because he hated obliging the black students. At one point in the play, he tried to explain himself, to defend his point of view by talking about his private life; he tried to attract sympathy from the audience (a largely white, middle-class one) so that his position would be understood. But in the balcony was a large school party of black students who felt very uncomfortable at being asked to understand a racist's point of view. They started laughing at him, while the audience sitting in the more expensive seats below remained silent and "understanding." There was more than one "character" being portrayed in the role of the janitor that evening; those characters were not all contained by the play on stage. They had a life of their own beyond the footlights.

I hope this story shows how precarious a character is in a play. A character is not "fixed." To think that a monologue will help define a character is misguided. A monologue means something only if it is part of the overall argument, if it is the result of the shifting play of points of view.

Character and Psychology as Functions of Irony

Let us return to our innocent student. We know he is innocent. We know from the principal's words that he is frequently in trouble and protesting his innocence. This time it happens to be true.

Before the principal made us aware of the past background of this character, we had a character of limited dimensions, simply one of two students accused of starting the fight. The best way to teach children about dramatic characterization is to demonstrate in this way, through improvisation and discussion, that a character is not one-sided, but part of a multi-dimensional, theatrical argument. Different points of view, shown by putting the character in a variety of contrasting situations, will slowly create a history and imply a future that bear on the present situation in which the character finds himself. It is possible to start with a single trait and see what others it leads to by testing it in different situations.

We have seen how this multi-faceted approach to characterization encourages and clarifies irony. This is especially useful, because I have found that younger students rarely think ironically. The student who gets into trouble a lot because he is treated as a scapegoat might be described simply as a "whiner" or a "squealer." What you must do, in such a case, is to help the students develop a scenario that makes sense from the point of view of the character concerned. We need to understand *why* he whines, *what* he intends to achieve by it, and *how*, as a point of contrast, the whining is interpreted by other people. This process enlarges the concept of "whiner" from a label that is slapped on someone, like the label on a pair of jeans, into a dynamic that helps shape a personality or is shaped by it. This is also what we mean by a person's psychology: not a single trait that traps someone into behaving in a particular manner—that would be a stereotype—but rather a set of values and beliefs, belonging not only to the person but also to his or her community. These all help determine the character's behavior.

To teach these lessons, ask the class for character ideas. If the students offer a set of fixed attitudes, begin to develop a plot that will both express and challenge these attitudes. Here is what an elementary class in Queens once offered me:

☐   A fierce cat named Tom.
☐   An aggressive bum named Walter.

And here is how we set them in context and gave them dramatic life:

Scene 1   Late at night, in the slums, Tom is disturbed by a singing, drunken bum, Walter. Tom hisses, spits, and scratches Walter's boots. Walter savagely kicks Tom. Injured, Tom slinks away, still fiercely.

Scene 2   The next day, Tom is smarting from the indignity of being kicked by Walter. His pride is hurt, so he is even more fierce than usual. He is so preoccupied that he does not see the bicycle wobbling along the cobbled street, and he is knocked down. Helpless, Tom lies in the gutter, filthy and bleeding. Suddenly, a pair of hands gently lifts him up, and we see this severely humbled cat looked after by the same bum who kicked him the previous night.

Notice how the first scene expressed simple attributes, but the second scene sought to challenge those attributes, to offer an alternative viewpoint. The crucial point at the end of Scene 2 was that the class decided that Tom did not recognize Walter. Instinctively, these fourth graders wanted to heighten the pathos by sharpening the irony. Tom started out fierce, then became helpless; while injured, Tom may feel fierce, even if not actually being fierce. The singing, drunken bum was aggressive; the sober bum was gentle. Walter is happy, drunk, aggressive, sober, and gentle—the same person! The two contrasting scenes expand the character traits of fierce and aggressive by making sense of them in the context of a rough neighborhood where kindness and cruelty coexist. To define Tom and Walter's psychologies without reference to the greater life about them would be to stereotype them.

Suspense occurs when you do not know something. Irony occurs when you know something but other people do not. We knew the student in the fight exercise was innocent; the principal did not, and indeed, had reason to think he was guilty. From Tom's point of view, there is the suspense of finding out who his benefactor is. From our point of view, there is the irony that we already know.

Irony is central to playwriting, so it is worth spending some time on this point. Encourage the students to give you examples from real life: "Can you think of a situation when you knew something about someone, about which they, or other people, knew nothing?" Here are some examples of dramatic irony that students might supply:

- ☐ I was talking to my best friend, and she thought she was going to get the lead in the school play. I already knew she had not been cast at all.
- ☐ My brother had done something wrong, and when my mother came into the room and asked me what happened, I decided to say nothing.
- ☐ My girlfriend's boyfriend was two-timing her, but she didn't know, and kept on giving him presents.

All these examples contain contrasting points of view that indicate a dramatic tension, a pressure that is laid on the characters involved. How characters respond to that pressure shows us what sort of people they are. What is missing from the students' scenarios are the feelings and mental attitudes that inform the characters' behavior—the reasons they acted the way they did.

Now, as we saw above, a single adjective will not supply the reasons for a character's behavior. The girl who thought she was going to play the lead in the school play could be described as arrogant—for two very different reasons:

1. Because she was not a good actress but desperately wanted to attract attention to herself and so imagined she was a good actress.
2. Because she was a good actress, but had let it go to her head so that she felt she was indispensable.

Building a character, therefore, must be a precise craft. The examples of irony that the class offers should be examined carefully so that we share the irony fully by understanding the opposing points of view. The girl whose boyfriend is two-timing her thinks that she is being loving, generous, and romantic—that is her character from her own point of view. But we also see her as foolish and self-centered, so much so that she blinds herself to what is going on. The irony works only if both points of view are dramatized. It is like completing an electrical circuit: the character sparks only if the two poles are connected.

Empathy with a character, therefore, does not mean imagining that we are that person, or that we think or feel exactly as she does. It means understanding the specific situations well enough so that we know why a character acts the way she does, even though she may not know why herself.

Character and Emotion in Action

By this stage, the students should understand that a character is not an adjective. A fierce cat, a foolish girl—these tell us nothing. There must be something behind the adjective. The cat is fierce because it helps him survive in the streets. The playwright must show the character acting in a situation that clarifies not only *what* the character is doing but *why*. Again, these matters can be viewed as answers to the question, *why*. Portrayal of a character is a matter of *how*. This means translating any adjective, state of mind, attitude, or belief into appropriate actions for that character. It is impossible to depict someone "feeling happy." It is possible to depict what the person is feeling happy about, because this immediately puts the character into a relationship with something or someone that results in a specific kind of happiness. Something happy has to happen. It's also possible, of course, to dramatize the results of an emotional state—such as Mandy's staying in her room because her mother had died—or the reaction of other characters to someone who is unbearably happy about something, which may be one of alienation. Look at both sides of an emotional state—cause and effect.

So, you cannot describe characters in terms of a feeling. How do we know what they are feeling? Any feeling has to be revealed through an activity or a result. There are many ways of feeling "cruel" or "kind"—as in *Hamlet*, sometimes the two are confused! If X is cruel—*why*? And *how* is it shown? It will be the action, or the way the person talks or reacts to those about him, that will reveal the type of feeling the author wants to convey. The same things apply to what a character believes in.

Exercise

□□□□□□□□□□□□□□□□□□□□□□□□□□□□□□

Dramatizing Feelings and Beliefs.

Here is a writing exercise for the class:

Take certain feelings or beliefs, express them in short-story form, and then make sense of them theatrically by finding the dramatic action and inventing the appropriate dialogue. For example: Greg was on his way home from school, nervous and depressed about showing his parents his report card, because they had said unless his scores improved, he could not go out for sports.

Start with an emotion, then add a name and a situation. Write it out simply, as in the above example. Find the point of dramatic action and draft a scene that will communicate the feelings you wish to. You are trying to get the students to realize and put into action the clash of perceptions that creates character and dramatizes emotion. There is a distinction between what one person feels about himself and what another person believes. Here are some other examples of a character's feelings or beliefs that you can dramatize:

Peter feels he is too stupid to pass the exam for college. (Try to dramatize the precise distinction between Peter's own perception of himself and someone else's belief that he is just lazy.)

Kendra feels ashamed at having to go to school in her sister's hand-me-downs. (How does Kendra compensate? Anger? Sloppiness?)

Molly is one of the popular kids at school but doesn't like to go along with everything the crowd does. She wants to remain her own person. (Consider how other people in other school cliques might view Molly. She considers herself her own person—do other people?)

Dennis is angry at the way the boss treats him, but he needs the job. (How can he express his anger without being fired?)

This last example illustrates the problem of dramatizing an emotion that must be kept suppressed or a feeling that must be kept secret. How do you translate an inner, secret feeling into an openly expressive action? How can a playwright help an audience see inside a character's head, know what a character is really feeling?

People do not go around with bubbles over their heads saying things like, "Despite appearances to the contrary, I am actually feeling ghastly because my mother has just died." Ask the class for ways of expressing hidden feelings, such as grief, through action. It is likely the most common device will be a marked change in behavior that defies expectations and provokes questioning. Just as our innocent victim alters his behavior to encourage people to believe in him, our grief-stricken character will turn from being the life and soul of the party into someone moody and unresponsive, or the shy and retiring sort may uncharacteristically draw attention by crying.

So what we find is that a person's external life, which may be assumed or which may be how he or she is perceived by others, is acted upon by some force, action, or event that draws out and makes public the internal life and points up atypical behavior in a character. The drama in a character does not lie in the tortured inner conflicts of his soul, but in the contrast between his perceptions of himself and others' perceptions of him. The more extreme the contrast, the more extreme the action to which the character is driven.

A stunning example of this is a play called *I'm Tired and I Want to Go to Bed*, by David Torbett, who was eighteen years old when he wrote it. It was performed in the 1983 Young Playwrights Festival in New York. The protagonist was a boy who failed at school but who felt inside that he was capable of great insights and of being a great success. In order to achieve this, he summons Mephistopheles, who duly arrives—in the form of the play's narrator, of all things! Mephistopheles invites the boy to travel to the Fourth Level of Existence, where success awaits him.

JEROME: How do we get there?

NARRATOR: The same way Doctor Faustus did—by cutting your arm. Here, take this dagger.

JEROME: That's a razor blade!

NARRATOR: Only on your level. On my level it's the key to ultra-existence. Go ahead, cut the vein.

JEROME: I'll bleed to death.

NARRATOR: You can't die. You're too powerful . . . too great. Cut yourself. Hard. (JEROME *nervously but somberly cuts his wrist*) Again. (*He does so again*) Good. It'll hurt for a little while, then the pain will go away.

JEROME: God, I hope so, because right now it hurts like hell. Look at all that blood. I've never seen so much blood before. It's making me dizzy. I've never felt this dizzy before. (*He lies on the ground and sings weakly*)

> Show me the way to go home,
> I'm tired and I want to go to bed.
> I had a little drink . . .

I can feel the life slipping out of me. (*He closes his eyes, pauses, then opens them suddenly*) There is nothing! Mephistopheles or whoever you are, there is nothing! You lied to me!

NARRATOR: I never lied to you. Only you lied to yourself. I don't even exist. (*Exit*)

One of the really remarkable aspects of this climactic scene is that we really believe that Jerome thinks cutting his wrists is the key to his long awaited success. The last scene takes us up to the moment of his suicide entirely from his point of view—but the Narrator's last line puts that point of view into perspective by challenging the boy's action with the objective, external reality—that Jerome has deceived himself. The complexities of Jerome's psychology are a neat demonstration of character as defined by argument (with himself, with Mephistopheles), character as clarified by irony, and character and emotion as expressed in an extreme action. Jerome's secret delusions about his success are shared, for different reasons, by another character. *Theatre involves the clash of two or more perceptions of the same thing*, even though there may be only one character on stage. When a change of perception occurs, a dramatic event has taken place.

Suicide is a favorite theme in teenagers' writing. Young people like to write about characters who strike out and behave in an extreme way. But the plays are often shallow and melodramatic, a posture, because not enough time is taken to show the walls inside characters, the barriers of perception and (mis)understandings between what they think or want and what other people think or want of them.

Character and Status

One of the best ways of teaching the difference between internal and external perception of character is to focus on status. Status defines how powerful characters are—not only in the social roles they play but in what they feel, and how much self-respect and self-confidence they have. It can also change from situation to situation.

Status is often conveyed by dress, appearance, or bearing. Medals and ribbons adorn military uniforms. The higher the status, the more special or rare the decoration. A single Victoria Cross pinned to the chest of a private will outstrip a host of campaign badges worn by a general. A unique dress worn by a woman at a fashionable party will endow her with great status—until someone walks in wearing the identical gown, at which point, the status of both women will plummet.

Ask the students for their own examples of status as expressed in dress. Encourage them to note the complications and contradictions, as well. The private with the Victoria Cross still has to salute the general. Dress can also be misleading, to the uninitiated: I remember as a small child in 1953 watching the coronation celebrations in my town. The Duke of Edinburgh was visiting, and he was welcomed by the mayor, who wore his ermine gown, tricorn hat, and gold chain of office. Needless to say, I got my characters mixed up, so unimpressed was I with the Duke's drab suit. I must have chosen to ignore the fact that the "Duke" in his ermine bowed to the "Mayor" in his suit!

This misunderstanding lies at the heart of how status works. The servant bows to the master, yet sometimes it is the master who metaphorically bows to the servant. A weak boss may have to beg his employees to do something, in which case the boss has lower status than the employees. Teachers face this constantly, varying their behavior, choosing to abide by or ignore rules of discipline, in order to retain high status with the pupils and command their attention and respect. Discuss with the students how status operates in different situations and changes from moment to moment. Examples:

☐   A good teacher who has high status with her pupils, has low status with her peers because she is the most junior member of the staff.

☐ The school bully has high status with the children in the playground but low status in the classroom because he's no good at his lessons.

Use this discussion to lead to improvisations and written scenes that show the characters' actions in relation to their status. A favorite example: A man, dressed in filthy overalls, looking like a mechanic, enters the classroom and proceeds to give a lecture on Shakespeare. Our expectations are upset. In context of the classroom, a grease monkey would have low status, but as soon as he opens his mouth, he becomes high status. Just as we analyzed the dramatic potential of an event by asking the question *why*, so we can examine the dramatic potential of a character by questioning the juxtaposition of a high-status action without expectation of low status.

It is helpful for young playwrights to think of a play's action in terms of the status, or power relationships, of the characters because it reminds us that a character is continually shaped by what he wants to do and what he is allowed to do. A character may want to scream out loud but is not allowed to do that. If he were to scream, this action would cost him something. Reiterate at this point that any dramatic action performed by a character involves a choice and costs that character something. You cannot make a character more important than the situation allows. Simply pushing up the emotional temperature of a scene does not push up a character's status. So the question is, if a character who has low status cannot be more important than the situation allows, how does the writer adequately recognize the integrity and worth of his feelings? Is a low-status character forever trapped into being the victim of his fate? Will the rebels and outcasts of young people's plays be forever jilted and betrayed, by Mephistopheles and others?

The Internal and External Sides of a Character

It comes back to perceptions and self-perceptions. One of the strongest impulses of young people's playwriting is to show a character who is weak, despised, handicapped, or lonely trying to attain some kind of power, control, or dignity. Students frequently identify with the underdog because they have an innate sense of justice and fair play. A great many of their plays protest on behalf of all low-status characters everywhere. In most cases, the characters remain relatively powerless because their protest backfires, or because it costs them life or liberty. A strong strain of despair exists in young people's writing, which I think reflects the disenfranchisement of children in our society. A typical scenario in their plays might be: A character tries to redress a grievance or gain some respect, and she will make an honorable attempt. She will fail and end up back where she started, beaten, but unbowed. Or she will end up in jail, defiant and angry. Or she will commit suicide. There will be a moment of temporary defiance and then the inevitable fall into powerlessness again.

This depressing view of justice reflects to some extent the students' view of life as they see it and live it. Many teenagers develop a low opinion of themselves. Some children don't give up at this point but begin to fight like Robin Hood, as an outlaw against huge odds.

What to do? I use Harriet Tubman as an illustration of someone who was treated as a slave because she was a slave, but who had in herself great pride. If you wish to make a chart of perceptions for this character, you would do it this way:

INTERNAL	EXTERNAL
Pride	Appearance
Determination	Subservient behavior
Beliefs	Job
Status (high)	Status (low)
Feelings, emotions	Religion
FREE	SLAVE

On the right hand are all the attributes dealing with her social role: her poverty, her relative lack of education, her subservience to her master, and the compensation of her religion. All are part of Harriet Tubman. But to dramatize only the External column would be to miss the point; it would be half the story. The Internal column lists all the attributes of her free spirit. Again, to dramatize only this column would be wrong and would miss the point entirely. Why is she so determined? Because she *is* a slave, and she *wants* to be free.

Use this Internal/External chart to analyze any character. It will give your students an increased sense of ownership and of being part of a serious dramatic tradition to do so. The point you are trying to make is that the playwright must depict both sides, because both sides are inextricably intertwined. Yet there is still a wall between them— the wall of perceptions.

Exercise

□ □

Dramatizing Internal and External Perceptions

Harriet Tubman's high and low statuses cannot be expressed simultaneously if they are evenly balanced. Instead, there is a huge gap between them. If the class understands this, ask it to imagine a scene where the two statuses clash, where a hole is knocked through that wall, connecting the two sides for a moment: Imagine a scene wherein Harriet Tubman, slave, comes into conflict with Harriet Tubman, freedom fighter. Here are some suggestions the class may offer:

- ☐ She gets angry and faces up to the master.
- ☐ She gets angry, but realizes that to show her anger could betray and endanger other lives.
- ☐ The master tries to break up a secret meeting of the slaves.
- ☐ She demands her freedom in the company of many other slaves.

Avoid sentimental sacrifice! If Harriet Tubman wants to force the issue, she must be very careful not to get herself chained up, whipped, or thrown into jail. If she has any sense, she will avoid being alone, for that would be sentimental and heroic—and dangerous, ultimately unproductive of her ends. Instead, she will choose an action that expresses her belief more accurately—her belief in the freedom of her race. She is more likely to stand up to the master as the representative of a whole host of slaves who are backing her up.

Young adults are very aware of status. They are sensitive to hierarchy, to the perks and privileges that come with higher status, and they are often ingenious at holding their own. A small kid may develop a quick tongue and sharp wit to use against a larger and physically more powerful peer. Possessions are exchanged and bartered according to their status value, and these values are often very personal. Someone may exchange a large slice of cake for a baseball card or a stamp. Clothes and bearing are minutely categorized according to status—walking tall, keeping cool, showing no emotion, or wearing a mask of permanent nervous aggression are part of a macho status. All things that are present in the school can help the students understand the dynamics and details of status. Have students observe examples of status in action throughout the school, note down the outward elements of it, and develop fictional characters from what they have seen.

Here is one final example of how a young playwright dealt with the walls of perception inside her characters, from *Half Fare*, by Shoshana Marchand, produced at the 1982 Young Playwrights Festival and published in the *Young Playwrights Festival Collection* (1983).

The following excerpt is the final confrontation at the end of the play between a fifteen-year-old girl and her divorced father. The girl wants her father to be strict, to lay down rules that will help govern her life. Her status as daughter is at war with her status as free agent, because her father refuses to do any of these things. Claudia does not want to be free; she wants to be George's daughter. She shatters the wall between them.

When reading the scene, try to see it in terms of the conflict between what each character wants from the other, and how the impasse finally forces a change in Claudia, a change that is so extreme in its implications that even at the brink she pauses, hoping George will give way. Notice how Claudia's status slowly rises, while George's slowly drops as the challenges to their respective walls become more and more intense until the crisis can no longer be avoided. The older generation is left weak and powerless; the younger generation walks out determined and free—but at a price. The key words in this scene are "do something" and "change," and they neatly sum up the point of this chapter. Character is defined by situation (What do I want/What do I do) and by dramatic action (change arising out of conflict).

CLAUDIA: Oh, I'm just stupid, I wreck everything.

GEORGE: *(He pulls her onto his lap, perhaps playing with her hair)* Well, what did you expect? You're much too young to make love to someone you don't know and expect to feel happy about it.

CLAUDIA: *(Pulls away, hard and fast)* Not right or wrong. Just too young. Is that all?

GEORGE: Look—if you know this is wrong for you, then why do you go and do it? *(For the remainder of the scene, Claudia must be played with defensive energy; no whining)*

CLAUDIA: I just thought it would make you—I don't know.

GEORGE: What does this have to do with me? This is your sex life.

CLAUDIA: George, everything has to do with you.

GEORGE: What?

CLAUDIA: I don't know. *(Tries to get away but he pulls her back strongly. She's still tensed)*

GEORGE: Yes, you do. Now what?

CLAUDIA: Evan wanted to go for a while before you came home.

GEORGE: So why didn't he?

CLAUDIA: I kept teasing and not letting go, and—

GEORGE: Why? You wanted him to stay? If you'd told me, we could have worked it out.

CLAUDIA: No, not that. I kept thinking you'd be home soon and I wanted you to know he was here.

GEORGE: What are you saying?

CLAUDIA: *(In sobs, but no whining)* I didn't want it to work out! I wanted you to catch me here with him. What do I have to do? What if I get pregnant? Are you going to hand me the abortion money and tell me to take the subway home? What if I'm with two naked men the next time you walk in? What if one of them is seventy-three years old? What if I'm making it with a goddamned thoroughbred horse? What are you going to do, George? George, you have to do something!

GEORGE: Just calm down a minute so we can discuss this like rational people.

CLAUDIA: George, I just told you everything. Now you know what's wrong, you can change it. You can stop me. You can be my father, George.

GEORGE: You're repeating yourself.

CLAUDIA: Please, George, you're supposed to fix it and make it better, you can do that now. I'll listen, I promise, George.

GEORGE: Claudia, I'm tired. You're tired. You're overwrought. Go to bed.

CLAUDIA: What are you? What kind of father are you, what kind of man are you? What kind of person? George, you're not, you're nothing.

GEORGE: I am thirty-seven years old, and I am quite happy with my personal life. Get that? You better get that, once and for all. Whether or not you believe it, I am perfectly happy the way I am. So you can just cut out telling me to change. I'm not interested. Change yourself.

CLAUDIA: No. It's not my job alone. Either you do something, or I'll do it. And I can't *do* anything around you, George. I'll leave.

GEORGE: Just calm down, for Chrissake.

CLAUDIA: I'll leave, George, I swear I will. You don't want to let me go. I'll leave, George *(chokes)*, do something! Please! *(No response. He stares in disgust and passivity. She sobs, runs to the bureau by the bed, jams clothes in a small backpack, and her sobs quiet down.* GEORGE *does not look at her now. She gets on her hands and knees and reaches under him to grab her shoes from under the table. She gets up slowly and heavily)* George, I'm going now. George? *(They stare at each other for a long moment, both sure that neither will go through with it. Then* CLAUDIA *walks quickly and quietly to the door, very controlled. She turns to face him. Very plainly)* George, I love you.

4

Improvisations

What Are Improvisations?

Improvisations (Improvs) are a spontaneous form of theatre. Actors are provided with a minimum of details about situation, character, and purpose, and take it from there. Some actors love them. Others find them an exquisite form of living hell. They are most often used as acting exercises. I have found, however, that they can be of enormous use to the apprentice playwright. In this chapter, we will look at some improvisational exercises for writers, as opposed to actors, and see exactly how a playwright can use improvs to improve his or her craft.

Improvisations in Playwriting

What is the purpose of using improvs in teaching young playwrights? First and foremost, improvs are a creative impetus, something to get the creative and imaginative juices flowing. Improvs can provide raw material and train the playwright in the judicious choice of what to use, what to cast aside. They are also a superb tool in the process of revision and rewriting. Improvs can be done either before the class sets out to write or after a draft has been looked at, discussed, and acted out. If a scene doesn't work, it is possible to set up an improv using the same situation and seeing what went wrong, or where greater potential lies.

Rule 1: Keep It Simple

The first and most important rule is *keep it simple*. Don't bewilder students or yourself with too many instructions about time, place, situation, character. Apart from sabotaging any spontaneity, the students will rightly suspect you have some planned agenda, a specific end you want them to reach. They will spend their energies trying to do what is right, rather than what might be true.

Beginnings, therefore, should involve three instructions only: Where are we? Who is there? and What are we doing? This leaves the *why* and *how* up to the people who will "write" the scene in performance.

Choose familiar environments. Improvisations for beginning playwrights should concentrate on a simple dramatic situation that involves their particular world. Later on you can stretch their abilities by suggesting more exotic environments.

Do not choose settings that restrict too many possibilities. Speeding cars and stuck elevators are both stock settings that do not allow for the entrance of new characters. This can impose good discipline on those who need to learn how to handle extended scenes with the same characters, but it is too limiting for students just learning how to use improvs in their craft.

Characters □ Used here, the word is slightly misleading. You are not presenting your students with anything like a defined character. Give the students simple instructions about each person's objective or intention, and leave it at that. You do not tell them how, or even if, they will achieve their goal. That is for the students to determine. Do not use adjectives or adverbs. It is enough to give them "teacher," "late student," "jilted boyfriend." Let the students create the characters they wish to write about.

Remember to alter the names of the participants to fictional names. This will free students of self-conscious restraint and tap their unselfconscious energy. Again, avoid the temptation to over-elaborate or add that extra bit of detail that might block the rush of energy that initially impels a student to get up and improvise.

Stage Directions □ The main stage direction for each improvisation should be an action, coupled with an intention. Example: You meet someone and proceed to disagree with that person. You provide the *what*; the students provide the rest.

Give the characters an entrance. It's more useful to the students than placing them in the center of the room and saying, "Right, let's go." An entrance gives the students a chance to think about the *who*, *what* and *why*, and to begin to work out the how, and it provides the scene with natural momentum.

Avoid literal props. A note can be mimed; bells, buzzers, and ringing telephones can be vocalized. A knock on the door should be provided by someone rapping on a desk, rather than the perilous "knock, knock." Some props, such as knives, should definitely be symbolized by something less immediately dangerous, but still potentially threatening, say, a wire coat hanger or a ruler.

Rule 2: Keep It Short

With beginners, you may well find that the initial enthusiasm to get up and perform evaporates quickly into embarrassment and frustration once they are on their feet. The second rule is therefore, not to expect too much too soon. Put students at ease with improvs that are not only simple, but short. The first one may last no longer than fifteen seconds. When told to meet in order to disagree, I have seen two students walk straight past each other, one offering a cheery hello, the other responding with a surly grunt. That was the extent of the Conflict Improv, but it made everyone laugh because of its simple, vivid honesty and theatricality. If the students resist the situation and do not really disagree, you will probably get meaningless exchanges about trifles—ten seconds of that kind of material is plenty, so end it then and there. Of course, you have to use your judgment and not pull the plug on a little scene that is actually developing into something.

Rule 3: Everything is valid, so long as it is real

This more commonly applies to actors, but it is a lesson playwrights need to learn to avoid self-indulgence. Everything that happens on stage during an improvisation is valid, must be accepted, so long as it is within the reality of the scene, and so long as the participants accept its reality. It can teach the apprentice playwrights that everything in their plays need not be the way the world at large sees it so long as it creates an internal logic by the acceptance of the characters. The instruction to "write only what is real" can be stifling to young imaginations and creativity—the challenge should be "write what you want, and make it real".

An example of this would be to have two old friends meet after many years. (These are the Characters and the Situation.) Each gradually imposes on the other certain facts. (Intention/Objective of the scene)

An extreme example of this exercise might proceed:

A: I see you've got yourself a new glass eye.
B: I have a stack of them now. Use them to play marbles. (B has accepted the glass eye, and now counteroffers:) Do you want a game? Or will your old war wound stop you from bending over?

A: You'll have to help me down. Once I'm down I can do anything. *(A accepts the war wound B has imposed on him)* Ready? I'll lean over and you can catch me. One, two. . . .

B: Wait a second. I'm wearing my favorite marble. I'll just put in this blue one, instead. *(Swaps his glass eye for another in his pocket)* Okay, ready. But watch it with your crutches.

If B had blocked, had rejected the reality of having a glass eye, the scene would have died. Because B accepted and responded to A's challenge with positive zest, their actions are quite valid.

This is an example of the kind of thing you would get from experienced actors. It would be as difficult to get this response from beginning writers as it would be from beginning actors. Nevertheless, the lesson we learn from this improv is to accept rather than reject whatever is offered, no matter how outlandish or unconventional. If the students accept it within their scene, you must too. Sometimes this reaction will come about not through quick thinking or inspired acting, but through simple panic at having to reveal emotions. One improv I used with schools was "Late For School", in which a mother who has just discovered that her husband has died in the night must cope with getting the children off to school. The reaction of the mother frequently would not conform to the norms of grief because the students were afraid of acting too emotionally. I have seen "mothers" drag their husbands out of bed (the desk), onto the floor, look down bewildered and coolly walk back across his body to the kitchen table. So long as the fiction is not shattered by giggles of embarrassment (appeal to both the participants and the viewers to take the scene seriously), the reality of the scene remains intact.

These moments of sheer panic are the kernels of truth in improvisations and in writing. People do not always respond in given ways. At some gut level, students will find this out and will discover that their view is valid.

Similarly, this exercise teaches the students that if they choose unusual material or scenarios, they must make it real to the characters so that the audience will accept it as real.

Rule 4: Refer to the students as writers, not actors

Do not worry about the surface quality of the acting. When teaching playwriting, I use improvs as an emotional release, to help students analyze behavior, to look beyond the commonplace, which may be unreal. Watching an inspiring actor perform an emotional scene is certainly an inspiration, but watching an inexperienced actor perform a scene that was written with truth, albeit self-consciously and perhaps clumsily, can be just as instructive.

After a scene, instead of asking, "What was Nancy like, acting the part of Griselda in that scene?" say, "What sort of character did Nancy write for Griselda in that scene?" Remember that writing an improvised scene means writing the stage directions as well: "What stage directions did Nancy provide that helped us realize Griselda was blind?"

To help reinforce that this character or that stage direction was crafted by a writer, I use a technique used in psychodrama. I stand next to the writer and put my hand on his or her shoulder while I ask the class some questions. "What did Nancy choose to write to show Griselda's feelings when she put her hand into the bag?" Then poll the group: "What would you have done at that same moment if you were writing the scene?" The point is that while you are acknowledging Nancy as the creator of the scene, you distance her from it by emphasizing the separate existence of the character she has written. Griselda becomes something more than evidence of someone's improvisational acting abilities. Griselda, not Nancy, now exists to be analyzed and manipulated according to the crafted choices of the young playwrights. Their comments will help Nancy objectify what she has written in the improv, and spur her on to a second draft, whether in improv or in writing. The second draft may well be subjected to a second reading for comment and further improvisation to generate new ideas or new ways of looking at the scene. Each time, the strategy is to help Nancy take responsibility for what she has created and to improve it.

You are thus giving the students a model for their own playwriting. Eventually, they will find their own individual methods of improvising to themselves, either silently in their heads, or out loud. (I know many successful writers who speak aloud the lines as they write them. A friend of mine thought his roommate was schizophrenic—until he found out he was a closet playwright!) Playwrights have to hear the words they have written, to know they ring true. Thus, the improvisations that the students practice now will become a basic tool for them later on.

Summary of Rules

1. Keep the instructions to a bare minimum. Just say *who, what,* and *why.* Avoid psychological detail. Do not ascribe any qualities to the characters: let the students write the situation by writing their own characters, and vice versa.
2. Keep it short.
3. Everything that happens is valid so long as the students accept it as real, make it real, and remain in role. Be careful not to insist on a conventional or predetermined reaction.
4. Regard improvisations as part of the process of writing, rather than as an acting exercise. Don't let the quality of the acting get

in the way of analyzing the choices made by the writers. Introduce the idea of revision and rewriting by referring to each improvisation as a further draft. Transform the spontaneity of the improv into a draft that can be reread and rewritten. Emphasize the craft.

Warm-up Activities

There are hundreds of ways to ease students into improvs. The books listed in the bibliography contain enough suggestions for a lifetime. With practice, the teacher will find out what works best and will begin to develop a technique that is more personal. Here is a warm-up activity I've found to be useful and suitable for all ages:

Have the students form a circle in an open space. The leader, perhaps the teacher, says his or her own name, then makes a gesture and a noise at the same time.

The student to the left copies the teacher, repeating name, gesture, and noise. The same student then says his own name, making a different gesture and noise. This continues around the circle, each person repeating what the person before has done before creating a new gesture and sound. Note: *It is important to remind people about the sound. They often forget.*

The fun of the game is partly to be found in inventing noises that are simple enough to imitate but at the same time not too innocuous. If someone utters a warcry and then does a somersault, then the next person must do the same thing. This is potentially embarrassing, especially if there are teachers or students who would normally shy away from such craziness.

I remember one school where the teacher, a rather portly, no-nonsense type, joined in so as to ensure cooperation and "undivided attention" from her students. Indeed, she positioned herself next to the class troublemaker, just to make sure she behaved herself. With each person in turn imitating the one before, the troublemaker was quick to recognize the opportunity presented her. When it came round to her, she screamed and did three push-ups! The teacher gamely followed suit.

Variation: Have everyone in unison repeat not only what the last participant said and did, but what every person has already said and done, building into something rather like "The House That Jack Built." This happens every time someone adds something new, so the exercise will take a long time to complete. Vary the tempi and volume for each repetition to avoid fatigue and boredom.

After the warm-up, analyze what has happened with the class. Ask, "Which sound do you remember best? Why?" Chances are, it won't simply be the loudest, but the cleverest. The group learns that the more distinctive the sound and gesture, the more they "belong" to the person who created them—this is exactly the point to make about characters in a play. Characters are memorable because they sound and act the particular way they do.

This exercise teaches young playwrights the importance of (1) observation, (2) distinctiveness of a person's character, and (3) the dramatic concept of a character's "voice," the sounds and actions that make a character distinctive.

Improvisations That Look at Conflict

Exercise

□ □

Conflict

Objective □ To explore the concept of conflict in drama, and what creates conflict.

Setup □ It often happens that students themselves introduce the idea of conflict in drama during the initial discussion of what is important to have in a play. This is very helpful because it leads into the first improvisational exercise, a very simple one to set up, yet rich with possibilities!

□ Ask for two participants. Scene: a school hall (or any similar thoroughfare which allows for the entrance of additional characters).

Instruction □ The first person to enter the space says something. The second person is to disagree with whatever the first person says.

You may also try this in a fixed classroom—have one student enter and sit next to another, and they proceed to disagree.

Analysis □ Here are some questions you might use to help the class analyze what went on:

□   Hands up, those who were interested in what happened. Hands up those who were bored.
□   Why were you interested/bored?
□   What would make the scene more interesting?

- ☐ Why did they disagree?
- ☐ Did they disagree?
- ☐ What might have happened just before the start of the scene?
- ☐ What could happen next?
- ☐ What sort of characters did they write?
- ☐ What sort of stage directions did they write, especially for entrances and exits?
- ☐ What third character could enter this scene, if we wrote a second draft?
- ☐ What dialogue and stage direction could be written to have one character keep the other from leaving the scene?
- ☐ Could this scene lead to violence?
- ☐ Why, or why not? Do we know enough about these characters to say?
- ☐ If it could, what would delay the moment of violence?
- ☐ What would defuse it entirely?
- ☐ How could this conflict lead to change or transformation in one or both of the characters?

Discussion ☐ This improvisation is deliberately open ended; anything may happen. The source of the conflict may become explicit, or it may remain tantalizingly vague. If it is too vague, however, it may lead the two writers into muddy waters, because neither knows what the other is talking about:

A: I hate you.
B: But why? I like you.
A: You know what happened last week.
B: But I never meant to hurt you.
A: I'll get back at you for it.
B: But I thought you would like him.

The sixth line hints at a cause for the conflict, but if it continues in this vein, the suspense wears thin. B is not really accepting the fact that A hates him/her. A is not offering anything substantial. One of them should offer a concrete reason for the dispute. Analysis helps the writers to be more specific. Once the reason for the conflict is made clear, it can be used to further effect. If A & B are two girls talking about a boy, and that boy suddenly enters, the two might well veil their remarks in generalities.

If the improvisation is very brief, ask the class how it might be made longer. As mentioned above, the characters must really disagree, must accept their conflict. The young writers will learn that it is not enough merely to disagree because that is what their instructions were. For a scene to be fully satisfying—to actors, to audiences, and to playwrights themselves—there must be personal investment in it. Emotional and mental satisfaction must be gained from expressing the disagreement as disagreeably as possible! That involves the writer's understanding and conveying the *why* of the conflict. Only then will the characters be more than incidental and have a right to be on stage.

Fighting for the right to remain on stage—this is a crucial lesson in playwriting. Characters should never be incidental but must justify their existence by pursuing their objective in the scene and throughout the play. Encourage students who are writing characters in improvs to fight for that right to remain on stage. This will help them learn to define the dynamics of the scene, to give their characters life and reason.

In other improvisations in this chapter, there will always be moments when characters are given the choice of remaining on stage, leaving, or returning to the action. If young playwrights learn early on that a character's presence on stage is precious and worth fighting for, then they will also see that a character's leaving the stage is an equally assertive action. It, too, implies a choice made by the character. Exits take nothing away from the drama; they contribute to it.

Sometimes this improvisation leads to the verge of a physical fight. This can be defused by your imposing a new rule on your writers— the nonviolent rule. As I pointed out in the exercise in chapter 3, the idea is to devise a spine-tingling scene based on those moments before a fight breaks out, because that is where the drama lies. A fight is not inherently dramatic.

Improvisations That Look at Feelings

Here is a small group of exercises designed to study how feelings can be dramatized, especially feelings that are not normally expressed but repressed. How are feelings made visible if they are meant to be repressed? These improvisations look at hate, anger, guilt, and frustration.

Exercise
□□□□□□□□□□□□□□□□□□□□□□□□□□□□□□
The Tower of Chairs

This is a very easy improvisation to set up, but it is challenging for the students. It is suitable for all age groups. This is a nonviolent conflict improvisation: the antagonist is a pile of chairs that can't even answer back, let alone participate in a fight.

Objective □ To discover ways of expressing powerful emotions realistically; to introduce in practice the concept of character status.

Setup □ Carefully build a tower of chairs. It does not matter if the tower collapses once or twice; in fact, it helps prove one of the points of the improvisation you will make later. Ask the students to help you make the pile. Make the tower as high as possible, preferably higher than the average student's eye level.

□ The tower of chairs is a person each student hates with a passion, someone on whom they would dearly love to revenge themselves, someone they would not normally be allowed to speak back to—but for now, decorum is suspended and they have the privilege of responding in whatever way they wish.

One by one, each student will address the tower, in order to vent the feelings they have for this person.

Instruction □ Respond to the tower. Address it in any way you wish.

It is important for the participants to maintain total concentration. It is hard to develop an honest anger in this situation, so the first two or three writers will risk a great deal. As time passes, however, as more and more students berate or curse the tower, it will begin to acquire a malevolence. It will be a receptor and repository of passionate feelings, even though it is passive, inanimate. By the time the fifth or sixth student addresses the tower, its very passivity will exude an active, deadly power. Urge the students who are watching the scene to keep their gaze on the tower, not on the student addressing it.

At some point, someone may touch the chairs. When giving instructions for this improv, it is important neither to forbid nor urge the students to touch the tower. If they ask, "Can we touch?" say, "I want you to respond to the tower. Address it in any way you wish. This is your chance to answer back." Ideally, the touching will happen as a response to the increasing frustration and anger the tower provokes. Usually, the moment when someone first touches the tower is an electric one. The chairs may shift slightly. The spell is in danger of being broken. Eventually, the tower might collapse at the smallest nudge, and the effect will be a shocking sense of relief, even of catharsis. But this relief will be felt only if the touching and collapse occur late in the process. In other words, the tower must gain status before it can lose it.

If someone touches the tower early on, and especially if it collapses, it might never gain status. It will simply be the scapegoat for some angry feelings with no depth. If the chairs really are responsible for some terrible acts, they could not be abused so easily—otherwise, revenge would be simple, and tyrants would never stand a chance. However, if this happens, it too can be useful. The students will see that their anger is weak, has no depth to it. You can analyze the improvisation in the same way as if it had gone its full distance, with the questions that will follow.

If no one touches the chairs, and the spiral of frustration loses impetus, suggest that someone address the tower with movement and touch instead of with words. I once saw a boy mumble an inarticulate and barely audible speech, as opposed to the loud and passionate ones that had gone before, and at the same time, he scratched the metal chairs with his fingernails. My hair began to stand on end. Then he gently nudged the bottom chair with his foot, and the whole group tensed visibly. After all the previous words, these tiny actions were very threatening: they finally pierced the layers of smug, resolute self-satisfaction that had grown around and protected the tower.

Analysis □ Here are some questions you can use to help the class analyze what went on.

□   Which seemed stronger, the tower or the person?
□   Did this change from person to person?
□   Whose speech threatened the tower most? Why?
□   Did any of the speeches adequately express the situation?
□   At what point did the tower intimidate you most as a group?
□   Did it seem difficult or easy to control the tower?

Discussion □ When it works, this improvisation illustrates the power of theatre to conjure a palpable reality out of the simplest elements. It relies on our imagination, for we know, and may have proved right from the beginning, that the tower is weak and vulnerable, not at all strong and intimidating. The moment of theatre that most suspends our disbelief is often the smallest or most economical combination of sounds and actions. In this case, it was the conclusion to a series of confrontations with the tower: it was a resolution that was fully earned by virtue of everything that had gone on before.

Young playwrights need to learn that they can craft their work in much the same way: they earn their big effects by carefully shaping what happens in advance. This will be further discussed in chapter 6, on the form of playwriting.

They also learned that silence and stillness, sometimes combined with physical size, can be strong elements in a character's stage presence as well as his or her status in relation to another.

The next improvisation develops this idea of how strong status can help provoke a character to reveal feelings that would otherwise remain repressed.

Exercise

□□□□□□□□□□□□□□□□□□□□□□□□□□□□□□□

The Principal and the Janitor

The chairs were inanimate; it was therefore a privilege to be able to address them as any character you wanted, regardless of whether they were alive or dead, a tyrant or a boss. In this improvisation, we are on more familiar ground. This is not wish fulfillment or fantasy . . . or is it?

Objective □ To train playwrights in the handling of shifting status as a function of conflict.

Setup □ Two volunteers. One is the principal, the other is the janitor. The scene: after school, in a corridor. The principal has locked himself out of his office, and needs to get back in. (It is up to your students/playwrights to determine the reason. Maybe he needs to get papers for an important school committee meeting.) The janitor is doing his job; for example, cleaning or sweeping.

□ The principal asks the janitor for the key. The janitor refuses.

Analysis □ Again, here are some questions you can use to help the class analyze what went on.

□   How did the students write their respective characters?
□   Did the characters retain their self-respect? Their status?
□   Did the stated action of the scene turn into something else?
□   Was the janitor in danger of losing his or her job?
□   Was the principal in danger of losing his or her authority?
□   What suppressed feelings were revealed? Why? How?
□   What did the scene tell us about the characters' lives outside the school?
□   What difference will this scene make for these characters in the future?

Discussion □ This scene relies on a clash of status. The principal's authority is challenged by the janitor's refusal to surrender the key. The janitor's refusal might endanger a job that depends on the principal's good will. The principal's inability to persuade the janitor might well reflect his or her overall ability to carry out his job.

The most obvious reaction for the principal is frustration. How does the principal deal with this? Frequently, frustration turns to anger, an attempted show of authority. It can then devolve into supplication, or bribery, or even puzzlement—after all, *why* is the janitor doing this?

In the first cases, the principal stands on his or her dignity, and on his or her status, which actually plummets. In the final case, in which the principal is not relying on status, the actions of the janitor become almost malevolent in their apparent motivelessness, and thus the sympathy is for the principal.

What about the janitor's role? Like the student who addressed the passive tower of chairs, the janitor now has a chance to hold the principal hostage, while he or she pours out every gripe and grievance the janitor can muster. He or she may tantalize the principal, shifting the subject of the argument away from the keys and offices. They may concentrate on school matters—Ah, well, I've been meaning to ask you about my pay raise. Despite the fact that the janitor has the upper hand in the scene, it may be funnier, subtler, if he or she retains some semblance of respect for the boss.

The principal's only recourse is to change the situation. How can this be done?

The point of this improvisation, as with the Tower of Chairs, is to open a Pandora's box of extreme feelings. It is astonishing how the improvisation can bring out latent infantile feelings. The frustrations often create a prototypical parent-child relationship. The principal becomes the pleading child to the parent/janitor. Sometimes the roles are reversed and the parent/principal pleads with the intransigent child/janitor. The most useful aspect of the exercise is that it teaches us that under pressure, a character reveals unknown strengths and weaknesses, whether that pressure is applied through design or accident. In the next exercise, we look at a more somber situation, with physical and emotional pressure brought into play.

Exercise
□ □
Cutting Bread

This improvisation is for more mature students.

Objective □ To dramatize an intensely dramatic situation through action as well as words.

Setup □ This is one improvisation where I break my own rule about naturalistic props. You will need a cutting board, a bread knife, and one or two loaves of bread.

□ Two people. One is suffering the loss of a family member. The second is a friend who has come to visit, to console. The scene is the kitchen of the first character's home. The action consists of three elements: (1) the first person needs to talk about what has happened, (2) the first person needs to cut bread to prepare a meal for the family, and (3) the second person is there to be supportive.

Equal weight must be given to these three actions and to the two characters. Try to avoid monologues. Given an intensely emotional scene to play, even when that emotion is likely to be private and quiet, students react out of embarrassment at revealing such strong feelings. Often their distress overwhelms the cutting of the bread—instead of cutting it to prepare a meal they stab at it and mangle it, using it as an *indication* of their emotional state, rather than the real thing. So instead of actions being an appropriate vehicle for the emotions, they are turned into a crude bandwagon for a display that is superficial and one-note.

If this happens, you need to emphasize the importance of cutting bread—it is as great a need for the bereaved character as the expression of grief. The action is simultaneous, but it is also separate. What you are searching for here is antithesis, not synthesis. The two actions do not necessarily contradict each other, but in their separateness, they may comment more subtly on each other than if one is totally subordinate to the other.

Analysis □ This section has been called "Improvisations That Look at Feelings." We are looking at feelings, not listening to them. Looking at the way the bread is cut will tell us a great deal.

□ How recently has the tragedy taken place? Is it, indeed, a tragedy, or a "release," which can still leave one numb?

□ What tone of voice was used by either person? Did this match or contradict the body language? How would you write stage directions to achieve this effect?

□ What is the emotional state of the bereaved person? Is it simple grief—or could it be tinged with something else . . . guilt, responsibility, relief?

□ Did the knife seem blunt, or sharp? Did this make a difference to the meaning of the scene?

□ How was the bread cut? Carefully?

□ Did the friend feel in a position of strength or weakness? How could you tell?

□ What sort of relationship exists between the two friends? Did this change or was it threatened during the scene?

□ What does the friend want? Is it simply to comfort or could there be another motive?

Discussion □ This improvisation tries to show how a strong, starkly defined situation can yield something enormously complicated. However awful we may feel, something else usually competes for our attention—in this case, feeding others and acknowledging a friend's presence. These two things counterpoint the tragedy. They are control factors that can help shift the scene away from monologue and lessen the tendency for the character to indulge in wordy grief or self-recrimination. Subsequent drafts of this same scene might involve the two characters in a conversation about anything but the death and the breadcutting might express the personal tragedy most eloquently.

Summary

These three improvisations—The Tower of Chairs, The Principal and the Janitor, and Cutting Bread—provide various situations in which the characters' feelings are suppressed or hidden for one reason or another. The characters want to speak but feel constrained, or they don't want to speak but feel obliged—what a perfect analogy for the pains and agonies young and even not-so-young playwrights go through in learning how to communicate! In each case, it is the situation that allows the characters to speak, not some arbitrary decision on the part of the characters—or the playwright.

The lesson for playwrights here is that feelings that are hidden or suppressed are likely to be so for good reason. They will be revealed only if pressure is carefully applied in such ways as to provoke a response. The skill is in finding the exact point of a character's vulnerability, and often this point is quite unexpected. It is like laying down a trip-wire for your character to stumble across and set off an explosion of feelings. The approach is oblique, and searches for an unusual or antithetical action that will force someone to reveal him- or herself against the conscious will.

More Exercises

The following improvisations will deal with dramatic devices already discussed.

An Improvisation on Point of View

Exercise
□□□□□□□□□□□□□□□□□□□□□□□□□□□□□□
The Gasman Cometh

Objective □ To illustrate the concept of point of view in playwriting, and how this can manipulate the audience's feelings and understanding of the situation. Despite the adult theme (alleged marital infidelity), it seems to work as well with younger writers as it does with older, especially in emphasizing the importance of a character's goals (What do I want?) and action (How do I get it?).

Setup ☐ Although this requires four people, announce that you need three. Select a fourth student as a surprise character after the improv has started.

☐ The scene is a kitchen. Mother is at home cooking dinner. The meal will not be ready for another twenty minutes. Her objective is to cook the meal. The son or daughter enters, really hungry and wanting to eat something immediately. The husband comes home from work. He thinks his wife is cheating on him and is determined to confront her. Make it clear that this is simply the husband's point of view—he may well be wrong. It is for the wife to decide for herself.

You might consider reversing the roles of the mother and father to challenge the stereotypes of housewife and the jealous working man. Whenever I have done this, I have found that the students assume the father is home cooking because he is out of work, not because that is where he usually is. This is another form of stereotype, but it does spice the scene a little more by adding bitterness because of the economic situation.

Whoever is cooking dinner is already in the scene. The child enters first and establishes the scene. Then the spouse enters. At some point, especially if the argument between the husband and the wife is about to reach the boiling point, send in your surprise character. If the wife is cooking, choose a male student; if a man, choose a female. This new character is from the gas company and has come to switch off the gas because the bill has not been paid in some months. *These are secret instructions for the fourth student only.* The gas cut-off is located in the family's home. This action also entails turning off the stove. The representative is authorized only to turn off the gas; he or she may not receive payment.

Analysis ☐ Here are some questions to ask about this improvisation.

☐ What sort of characters were written for the mother, child, father, and gas company representative?
☐ Who has the most authority in the family, and over what issues?
☐ Did each character try to achieve his or her objective? Who succeeded and who failed? Why?
☐ From the point of view of the characters, did that person behave reasonably in trying to achieve the objective? Did his or her behavior ever become unreasonable? Why? Try to place yourself in the shoes of each character here, seeing it from each subjective point of view.

☐   Did anyone in the kitchen use any cooking implement as anything but a tool? When? How?
☐   The scene began with four different but perfectly reasonable
objectives that tended to contradict one another. What did the
scene end up becoming?
☐   Which character interested you most?
☐   Take each character in the scene and discuss how you could
write the next scene of the play—from each point of view. What
could the overall play be about?

Discussion ☐ There are so many variables in this improv that you
can conduct it over and over again and still come up with surprises.
A great deal depends on how strongly each student pursues his or her
objective. If the student writing the child creates a bratty kid who insists
on staying in the kitchen to nibble on whatever food is available, the
character of the father may be so intimidated that he will find it impossible to confront his wife. Or he may order the child to leave the
room, in which case the child really does need to fight to remain on
stage, especially when the gas representative, even more than the parents, threatens his objective, which is to eat.

Often the child will get involved in the parents' argument. This is
why it is useful to let everyone know in advance what each person's
objective is—it gives the students more options to play with. I once did
this exercise giving the characters their objectives secretly. It did not
work. For the student writing the accused spouse, it is more productive
to be aware of possibilities, to be advised of the accusations that will
be leveled, so that she can more carefully determine what she says
and how she behaves. For example, does she use the knife in a way
that says she is innocent or not? What other clues are there to her guilt
or innocence? Sometimes the student writing the mother never makes
up her mind. Sometimes she does, but her decision is contradicted by
other things in the scene, possibly by the reaction of the husband, or
the child's testimony.

Sometimes the father will need to be reminded to pursue his goal
more quickly and firmly, as this will prepare for the argument over
the gas bill.

One of the points of this exercise is to show how four characters
may reasonably pursue their objectives in such a way that their very
rationality produces a completely irrational situation. The momentum
toward change is deliberately built into the characters' contradictory
needs. If there is no change, then the scene collapses into a round of
endless, pointless arguments. Someone has to give way, or dominate.
This is the point of the last question of the analysis: take each character
in turn and discuss his or her point of view as if they were the principle

character in the play. A terrific anecdote from the fifties exemplifies this. A resident production of *A Streetcar Named Desire* was planned for Chicago, and a long-out-of-work actor was hired for the part of the doctor, who appears only at the very end of the play, and who has few lines. When his family asked him what the play was about, he responded, "It's about a doctor who comes to New Orleans because he's received a phone call from a young lady whose sister is having a nervous breakdown." This does not mean each character in a play has equal significance, of course. But for the purpose of this exercise, it is useful to examine all possible handlings of the plot, to look at each character and his or her point of view. What would the next scene be? This questioning will prove that from one situation, there are many, many different plays to be written. It all depends on your point of view.

An Improvisation Manipulating a Point of View

Exercise

□ □

Green People

Objective □ To train playwrights to support their plays' themes by manipulating the audience through point of view.

I use this improv with all age groups. It is very simple, and it teaches two important points:

1. It shows the difference between writing for the stage and writing for the camera.
2. It helps students understand that they must not assume an audience knows what the playwright knows.

I developed this exercise after reading a play by seventeen-year-old Genevieve from New York. In it, she had a character watch someone else turn green (literally) right before the audience's eyes. I asked her, "But how does the audience know he's green?" Genevieve answered, "Because the other person says so." I said, "But will the audience believe him?" and proceeded to make my point with the following improvisation.

Setup □ Two volunteers. A will write the character who is seeing people turn green. B is a friend whom A has come to warn of this phenomenon.

☐ A enters to B. While A is describing this frightening experience, he notices that B is slowly turning green, right in front of him.

Analysis ☐ Here are some questions to ask the class following the improvisation.

☐ Hands up, those who believed green people were outside.
☐ Hands up, those who believed A was deluded and was hallucinating.
☐ Did character B really turn green, or was this another hallucination?
☐ If the whole point of this play is that people really are turning green, and that B really is turning green, how do we make this point? How do we convince the audience about all those green people offstage?   .

Discussion ☐ The first draft of the scene usually ends with the scales of credibility tipped firmly against A. Sometimes the class will give A the benefit of the doubt so far as the people outside are concerned, but with the declaration that B is also turning green, it becomes easier to dismiss the whole thing as a figment of an overworked imagination. A is obviously going insane!

However, the whole point of this exercise is to force the credibility gap shut, to force the audience to suspend its quite reasonable disbelief. The last question in the analysis is crucial for young playwrights: suppose the playwright wants the audience to believe people really are turning green in the streets, and furthermore, that someone is changing color right before our eyes. How do we convince the audience that A is telling the literal truth? How can we know for certain that B is turning green?

Suggested answers will probably include the use of green light or makeup—someone once recommended suspending a bucket of green dye above the stage and tipping it over B!

None of these answers is suitable for the theatre. Consider films like *The Elephant Man*, which involved very elaborate make-up for John Hurt, or *The Wolfen*, which represented the wolves' point of view by shooting with cameras traveling at high speed about two feet above the ground and with colored filters that changed the human picture of the world into something wolflike, or, of course, "Star Trek", which does all of these things (including green people!) extremely well. If the improv were a film, one could represent the truth of A's point of view with special effects, and apprentice playwrights are still going to think in terms of movies or television until they learn the power of words. Discard the special effects and one has the point of view of B, who is not seeing green people. The camera becomes the characters' eyes.

When we speak of the magic of the theatre, however, we mean live performance. What suspends our disbelief is the behavior and language of the characters—no more, no less. Technical effects should support, not substitute for, the actors and the script. In the theatre, the audience sees things as they really are; the only visual aid that changes what we see is the imagination.

This discussion should help students understand that they must build belief in the greenness of B by rewriting the dialogue and stage directions, not by trick effects.

Ask the class for suggestions on rewriting the scene. Should A be more upset or frantic, or perhaps more calm and rational and therefore, ostensibly, believable? But madmen often seem quite credible.

Should the scene then concentrate on B? In the first draft, audience empathy was with B, sharing his skepticism of A's story, even while it may have sympathized with A's madness. The second draft must break this empathy. Instead of sharing B's point of view, the audience must become skeptical of it and share A's point of view. In other words, the writer has to dramatize B's greenness before expecting an audience to accept A's bizarre allegations. This is similar to building belief in monsters, but in this case, the monster is on stage and looks ordinary enough. A's reactions on their own are not enough; they must be complemented by a strong, but not crude, dramatization of B's own "monstrosity." How do we do this?

I usually ask the same participants to redraft the scene. I whisper to B that he should "Act green, be green, in whatever way you wish. Think green!" Sometimes I illustrate this by whispering, "Try locking the door after A enters. Make sure we see you, but A doesn't. You could act a little strangely, close the curtains, offer a green-colored herbal tea. Things like that."

The second draft often quickly reverses the effect of the first. It is hard for an audience to identify with a character that writes "green" dialogue and "green" stage directions. The scene is now weighted so that we believe A more readily; and students can understand that this happened not by rewriting A's part, but B's.

This second draft can also be wonderfully strange and powerful. You will find that the most successful redrafts are those in which minimal behavioral traits are just the smallest bit offbeat—B taking a pause slightly too long before replying to everything A says, or an insistence on something trivial. ("Do sit down. No, not that chair, here sit in this one. I want you to sit in this chair. No, not that one, come on and sit in this one here.")

Food was once enormously useful in this scene, and could be again. I conducted a terrific version of this improv in New York for a teachers' workshop. B was sitting and listening to A, and as she listened, she reached down and picked up a brown paper bag. Without taking her eyes off A, she reached into the bag and pulled out a slice of green melon which she proceeded to eat. In this case, the teacher had offered her own lunch as a prop and the result was an hilariously appropriate stage direction!

This is also a very good lesson for young playwrights in making even the strangest situation absolutely real, so that the audience would not dream of doubting what it is—or is not—seeing!

The most important lesson for young playwrights to learn from this exercise is the power of manipulating a point of view. They learn that this manipulation has to be contained in the dialogue and then in the acting of the characters. In a curious way, all things begin as equals on the stage, which is a neutral space until something happens. A space in which anything can happen. Neither you nor the students can assume, as Genevieve did, that what someone says on stage is true. The truth, or the falsehood, has to be dramatized. That is what the craft of playwriting is all about.

5

□□□□□□□□□□□□□□□□□□□□□□□□□□□□□
□□□□□□□□□□□□□□□□□□□□□□□□□□□□□

Writing Exercises

■■■■■■■■■■■■■■■■■■■■■■■■■

The greatest barrier to all forms of writing is usually topic choice. An improvisation or brainstorming session will help overcome this, although a lively discussion sometimes provides some unsuitably melodramatic material that students cannot control in their writing. In one workshop I conducted in Brooklyn, some students agreed on the following image as their best starting point: "A luxurious house; an elderly woman with blood on her arms walks out dazed." Well . . . *that* play never got written! When I compared this idea with what they subsequently wrote, it was striking how the best plays were about low-key subjects, such as those drawn from the students' own experiences, hopes, and desires.

Warm Up Exercises

The following ideas are warm-ups based on the students' having to think about themselves. These can be used at the beginning of a session or as ice breakers for those whose enthusiasm for talk and improvisation suddenly evaporates when they are faced with paper and pen.

Exercise
□□□□□□□□□□□□□□□□□□□□□□□□□□□□□
Five-Minute Biographies

Objective □ To encourage students to look for experiences or emotions in their own lives that they can then use in their playwriting.

Write an autobiography in five minutes. General things, nothing too personal. Share with a few others in the class.

Draft at least two character sketches from the ideas from your own and other people's autobiographies. Add fictional names and fill in some details for each character under headings such as "Likes," "Dislikes," "Clothes," "Possessions."

Use these character sketches as the basis for a small scene . . . just a few lines of dialogue.

To make it easier to share these scenes among the class, try to give everyone some carbon paper.

Then use these short scenes as the basis for some improvisation to lead to more writing, and then further improvisation to develop each successive draft—each time expanding and qualifying what has been discovered about the characters. Revision and rewriting are based on performance; each new improvisation/draft leads to new possibilities and discoveries!

Alternative Exercise ☐ This time, instead of writing about yourself, try writing about someone you really like (or used to like), or hate (or used to hate). Proceed with the exercise as above, but always remember that for characters to be real, you have to be fair to them.

The point of this variation is to engage these characters in a tense situation that may dramatize why the authors particularly like(d) or hate(d) them.

Exercise

☐☐☐☐☐☐☐☐☐☐☐☐☐☐☐☐☐☐☐☐☐☐☐☐☐☐☐☐

Secrets and Confessions

In a group discussion, students say three things about themselves.

Then, ask the students to write down three more things that they do not want to share with others. Promise that absolutely no one is going to see what they have written. It is their secret, and will remain so. This may be the first time they have been asked to write something in class that they will not have to show anyone else. It may also be an introduction to journal writing.

These secrets may then become the material for a play, if they are later incorporated into a fictional context. Encourage students to create characters with their own secrets, and slowly build character sketches from them.

The point of these exercises is to help students value their own life experiences and use them in playwriting. Demonstrate through discussion and improvisation that things kept private, confidential, or secret are potential sources for drama. Secrets are hidden or suppressed facts—but they may also be confessed, and it is this tension that is dramatic.

Exercise

□□□□□□□□□□□□□□□□□□□□□□□□□□□□□□□□

Fantasy and Dream Letters

Objective □ To help students discover how to make their dialogue real, from character to character.

This exercise uses the quality of the human voice inherent in letters, as a direct lead into playwriting. One of the common weaknesses in young playwrights' work is that all the characters sound the same—stiff, lifeless, wooden. Yet when we write letters (especially when we write a letter asking for something we want or need), we hear our own, real voices.

Write a letter to someone—imaginary or real—and ask for something you desperately need. The letter has to explain the reason you need it, and it must put forth a compelling argument.

Then swap letters with a partner. The partner has to reply to the letter in the negative, also giving reasons for the response.

Swap back to the original letter writers and continue the argument.

Keep swapping. The partners must not grant the request until they are fully satisfied.

Proceed to scene writing by transforming the letters into dialogue.

One amusing example from a Vermont high-schooler began:

Dear God:

Eve and I are desperate for some clothes. . . .

God replied:

What possible need could you have for clothing. The temperature never goes below 80 degrees. However, I would be happy to give you bigger fig leaves.

Your God

Finally, after the Devil had offered some threads in exchange for their souls, Adam and Eve got what they wanted:

Dear God:
Thanks for the clothes. The Levis were a perfect fit.
Your friend,
Adam

Variation ☐ The first letter is now from a fantasy character, such as a creature from another planet, who desperately needs something from you, a human being.

This reverses the usual role of the fantasy character who grants humans their wishes. Dream plays are useful in widening the scope of a young playwright's language and subject matter beyond that of television parameters. Students enjoy writing if you present them with challenging ideas for scripts—or help them develop challenging ideas. Let them discover new possibilities by reading extracts from Strindberg's *Dream Play* and *Ghost Sonata*, and Calderon's *Life Is a Dream*, to name but a few.

Collaborative Writing Exercises

Fantasy letters involve a simple collaboration between two people. This section will offer some other suggestions for collaborations among the whole class. They are an ideal way of encouraging the weaker writers in the class to incorporate their suggestions, verbal or improvised, into the group creation. It is important for the teacher to organize a group-writing project carefully, for there is a danger that the most vocal students might dominate, and that individual contributions will not be respected. Notice how many times each student speaks during a lesson, and to whom. This awareness must be transferred to the whole class so that everyone recognizes what individual members do. Only then can a genuine ensemble spirit be reached. This is why, with the exception of the Collaborative Writing Game, I never move straight into a group project. Instead, see what each person produces on his or her own. One will write about the death of his grandmother, one about King Arthur, and another about a flying horse. In schools with large ESL populations, the group play may become a combination of words and mime. These adjustments, made by the group, are possible only if you have first allowed the students to reveal themselves on their own and accept the ways in which they have chosen to present themselves in their introductions (see chapter 1).

Once the group has an idea of what individual members are capable of and have committed themselves to a choice of topic, let them test their investment in that topic with improvisations in subgroups. These improvisations (in groups from two to six, and each student takes one role), allow the students to experience the topic, to feel their way into writing. This is a time when tape recorders could be useful. A transcription of a small group improv quickly transfers material to the page and solves a major problem: Because writing is so slow in comparison to thinking and speaking, the censor inside each person's head has a greater chance to block verbal inspiration. We constantly strive to be correct, and we correct what we might spontaneously say. In a group play, all that many more censors are at work. Transcriptions, though laborious, preserve the fresh, relatively uncensored material of the improvisation.

Exercise

□ □

A Collaborative Writing Game

This is a very simple exercise for all ages. There are two versions of it.

Version One: Collaboration on Its Own

Tell the class that you are all going to write a scene together. Decide on a setting, two or three characters, and an opening situation. Put all this on the blackboard. Ask everyone to copy this down and remind the students to put their names at the top of the page.

In a workshop in Flint, Michigan, we decided on the following:

> Scene. Health Club
> Characters: Fred, Jack (a dead body)
>
> (Fred finds the body of Jack)

Decide on an opening line of dialogue. In this case, we all agreed Fred would say, "Good Lord! What happened to you?"

Everyone writes a reply for any second character they would like.

After they have written the second line/speech, everyone swaps scripts with someone else and writes the third line/speech (presumably Fred's rejoinder) on that person's script. Swap again, this time with a different person, read that new script, and continue the scene, each time writing just one more speech or line for the appropriate character. Encourage students to write stage directions and introduce new characters, if they wish. The only rule is—one speech at a time.

This exercise is similar to the one in which each person adds a sentence to a story as it is passed around a circle. The difference is, with playwriting, lines of dialogue vary greatly in length. So rather than passing scripts around a circle and risking a delay while someone writes a long speech and someone else writes just one word, encourage the students to swap with whomever is ready and try to swap with as many different people as possible.

This exercise can go on as long as you want. You could spend ten minutes on it and then announce that the students have to end the scene; or you could stop the swapping, return each script to its originator, and ask people to continue on their own.

I like to give people the chance to read one another's scripts, to see how their contributions have fared in the hands of their peers—this will prepare them for the time they have to let their work go into the hands of director and actors! So, I may freeze the writing but ask the students to continue swapping; this time they may read the scene but not add any more dialogue. Eventually, I return the papers to their respective owners and share a few versions with the class.

Version Two: Collaboration as a Follow-Up to Improvisations

Use this version as a follow-up to an improvisation so that the scene becomes a development of an idea the class has been investigating. I often do this one after the Conflict Improv (see page 45, Ch. 4).

The setup for this exercise is the same as for Version One. The difference is that the scene now has a specific direction to it because it should answer some of the points raised in the improv. This means that the scene will be less random than the one written in Version One, even though written by many hands.

In Detroit, we did a version of the Conflict Improv in which a girl, Lynn, refused to go out with a boy, Eric. So, during this improv, we looked at the questions why did Lynn refuse Eric, and how would Eric deal with this—what would this do to his status, and what would he do to preserve his status? Although only the first question was articulated and given to the students as a starting point, the other questions became part of the improv. We delayed the entrance of Lynn, giving the student writing the part of Eric, and another student, writing a friend of Eric's (John), the opportunity to start exploring these questions. Then, with Lynn's entrance, there was an opportunity either to confirm what the boys had said (usually about her character), or to completely change what the audience had believed to be the truth. As with the Playground Fight exercise, the audience's—and the writers'—perceptions may be altered unexpectedly.

Scene. At Mike's house
Characters: Eric, John

(Eric and John are at the keg line)

ERIC: I wonder where Lynn is?

Uses of the Collaborative Writing Game

This exercise teaches several things:

1. It neatly introduces the conventions of layout.
2. It helps brainstorm themes or characters for a longer play.
3. It overcomes writer's block by constantly supplying a fresh speech to which one responds.
4. It encourages characters to adopt individual voices and different, surprising points of view.
5. It stimulates young playwrights to take more control of their writing.

The third and fourth points especially are for students who are just beginning to write plays. The exercise keeps them on their toes as they have to respond quickly to whatever is given them. The exercise is also anonymous, so weaker writers will feel more secure with whatever length of exchange they feel comfortable, and it also offers more insights into characterization: characters do not behave predictably, sometimes "mystery characters" are introduced at the most inopportune moments.

There are some negative aspects to the Collaborative Writing Game which are as useful, in their own way, as the positive aspects. One is having to face writer's block alone, without someone else's written scene to respond to. I say to a class, "When you write on your own, imagine that you pass the paper back and forth to yourself—try to stand in for each character and then stand back and look at what that character has just written as if it were a completely fresh speech which you have never read before. Think of writing plays as swapping your paper back and forth between your characters."

Another negative aspect is that, of course, there is no real control over the progress of the scene. Each speech is written in a contextual limbo and is vulnerable to being developed in ways no one expected. While frustrating at first, this compels young playwrights to keep themselves open to more possibilities for their characters than they might have considered on their own. It is a creative problem that forces students to take responsibility for their scene, and write it with an awareness of its overall tone and structure. In other words, the very thing that is bad about the Collaborative Writing Game is the very thing that forces students to respond as individual artists with their own voices.

I once did this exercise with an after-school group of more experienced writers. They absolutely hated it! It completely frustrated their sense of controlling artistry and craft. If you find this happening, you will know that playwriting has ceased to be a Game and is starting to become an Art.

Character Exercises

Several exercises can get students to work on developing characters in their plays. A few are outlined below.

Biographies and Inner Monologues

Writing monologues is often used to start students off in playwriting. As I explained in chapter 3, I think this is a mistake, as it can lead to one-sided characterization. It can, however, become a valuable exercise after the first draft of a play has been written. With the first draft, the characters have already been roughly defined by the basic situation. They have at least been put into a context. Working now on biographies and inner monologues will serve to highlight the details and test the characters in circumstances that have some bearing on the playwright's overall concept. This exercise is like a laboratory experiment, with the playwright mixing in different ingredients to see their effect on a par-ticular situation—but you have to choose the basic substance first (the play's situation) before you can test it with a variety of elements (the characters' histories and inner lives).

Exercise
□ □
Inner Monologue

Suppose a play's situation concerns parents and children. Write an inner monologue for the child, choosing from the following possibil-ities: You are walking home from school and (1) you have been sus-pended, (2) you have spoiled your mother's scarf, (3) you have lost the money your parents gave you for the school photographs, (4) you've failed a math test for the fourth time, and (5) you've had a fight with your best friend.

These monologues will not exist in a vacuum, even though the situation suggested is very slight. There is a situation, and the students will have to make certain choices, such as what kind of relationship does this character have with his or her parents?

Another version of this exercise would be to have students observe strangers, noting their appearance, behavior, and ways of talking. Then have them construct biographies of these people. Armed with the bi-ographies, the students can then construct inner monologues for these new characters.

Exercise

□ □

Living Sculptures

This exercise will test students' powers of observation—one of the playwright's most vital tools.

Arrange a friend of yours into his or her most characteristic pose, and see if others agree with it. Then see if you can arrange the same person into *your* most characteristic pose. Add other living sculptures into a group arrangement, everyone based upon their most obvious bodily attitudes.

Write a scene based on this group of living sculptures. Then alter the attitudes subtly—the tinier the difference, the better. How has the script changed?

This exercise is based on observation and analysis of oneself as much as of others. The class will interpret the sculptures differently, and this helps the students learn the importance of clarifying points of view and to understand the significance of even the smallest variations in body language.

Exercise

□ □

Embarrassing Moments

Think of an embarrassing moment in your life. Write a private confession about it—and don't show it to anyone else. Think what could have happened instead to have saved you from embarrassment. Write the same. Do the same for imaginary characters.

This exercise has a therapeutic effect because it allows students to correct something that went terribly wrong. It also gives them experience in distancing true material.

Reverse the exercise: Write a scene about something that normally goes well, but now goes awry.

By concentrating on the students' personal experiences, you help them to feel their imaginary characters' feelings more intensely, which makes the characters more real. This is particularly useful when writing about a character's suppressed feelings.

If All Else Fails . . .

If students still have a great deal of trouble moving into writing anything at all, then try using one of these Jump Starters.

Exercise

□ □

Continuing Scenes

Choose a topic and improvise around it. On the blackboard put:

Topic:

Improvisation:

Scene:

Characters:

Stage Directions:

Ask the class to continue the scene after the improvisation. This can also be used as a tool for revision when a scene just doesn't seem to work.

An alternative is to do what the Creative Arts Team, based at New York University, do. They have different beginnings for scenes dealing with different situations. They print these Starters, including a small vocabulary chart defining any words that might cause difficulty, on attractive sheets that fit into a student's folder. Team members do a workshop based on one of the situations covered by one of the Starters. Then they give each pupil a copy and invite them to continue writing the scene. Here is an example, including the student's contribution (which starts after the words "Begin here"):

THE NOTE

(Parent is in the living room, searching)

PARENT: Where are my car keys?

CHILD: *(Calling, off)* They're on the table by my books.

PARENT: What are my car keys doing on the table in the first place? *(Picks up keys)* Stuck in all this junk. Who put them there?

CHILD: Not me . . . It must have been someone else.

PARENT: Nobody's home but you. *(The parent picks up the keys. Parent notices a piece of paper on the table and begins to read it)*   .

CHILD: *(Entering)* Hey, great, you found your car keys. Catch you later. I gotta make tracks for school.

PARENT: Just freeze right there!

CHILD: Huh?

PARENT: *(Holds out paper)* Is this your writing?

CHILD: I don't think so . . . I mean I don't remember . . . it could be mine. Let me see it. *(Parent holds the note away from the child)*

PARENT: But it's not your writing, and it's not mine, either. But someone tried to *forge*¹ my name to it.

CHILD: Ah . . . it looks like your handwriting . . . maybe you just forgot you wrote it. You know how you forget things. Let me see it. *(Again, the parent refuses² to give it to the child)*

PARENT: Dear Mrs./Mr. Smith. Please excuse _____from the *assignment*³ due today . . .

CHILD: I've gotta go to school. I'm gonna be late . . . *(Child tries to leave. Parent prevents⁴ child from leaving)*

PARENT: (Grabbing him, reading note) "_____ has been really sick since last Thursday when _____broke his/her leg? And yesterday _____ got the mumps, chicken pox, and the measles. So _____won't be back to school for one week. _____will be in *isolation.*⁵ Please do not call my house. Yours truly, _____. Who write this note? Tell me. Who wrote this note?

CHILD: Don't get mad. Don't get mad.

VOCABULARY
¹ forge: signing someone else's name.
²refuse: to say no; to deny; reject.
³assignment: lesson; homework.
⁴prevent: to keep from happening; to stop
⁵isolation: to set apart, to be alone.

BEGIN HERE

FATHER: What do you mean, don't get mad. Who wrote it?

CHILD: I don't know.

FATHER: I'll find out who wrote it.

CHILD: I got to go to school now.

FATHER: Wait, you're not going anywhere, until I find out who wrote this note.

CHILD: I don't know who wrote it.

FATHER: You told me not to get mad, now, who wrote it?

CHILD: My friend wrote it because he wanted me to play hooky with him.

FATHER: I'll come with you to speak to the teacher about this.

Exercise

□ □

Notes Toward Writing a Scene

Instead of improvising a situation as a way of understanding it, this exercise seeks to improve the quality of students' thinking by writing brief notes in answer to a series of simple questions. The class can do this sitting in fixed desks, if necessary; in this exercise, there is no movement, no improvisation, no randomness, no noise! With a normal-sized class, however, it is best to divide the pupils into groups of six.

Exercise □ Discuss truancy. Everyone writes down one good reason for cutting school.

Read your reasons to one another in groups and write down what others say. You should now have a maximum of six reasons (some may be the same), including your own.

Choose two of your favorite reasons. Share them with others—you may change reasons, if you wish.

Next, write down the people to whom you would reveal those reasons. For example, if someone's chosen reasons are meeting a friend and avoiding a fight you might add "friends" to the first reason, and "teacher" to the second—these are the people to whom you reveal the real reason for cutting.

Now, write down your excuse—the lie—for cutting, each lie being related to each of the two true reasons. Add the person to whom you would tell this lie. You might end up with:

1. Truth: meeting a friend (to friends); lie: helping my mother (to teacher).
2. Truth: avoiding a fight (to teacher); lie: going on a school trip (to parents).

Would the people to whom you told the lies ever find out the truth? How? What happens then? Choose one of the sets of truth and lie, and answer those questions for that specific scenario.

For example, we might apply those questions to the following scenario:

Truth to teacher: Lie to parents:

Avoiding a fight.   Going on a school trip.

And you might answer those questions in the following way: The parents find out the truth from the teacher, who confidentially informs them that their child is being bullied.

What happens next?

The parents decide not to tell their child so as not to embarrass him or her. Because they are so keen on their child's education, they agree to a transfer to an alternative school. They do not tell the child the real reason. *They* make up an excuse (lie), such as saying that the alternative school has a special program that they like.

Because this step-by-step question-and-answer process takes a good fifteen to twenty minutes, it means the class has time to think

about the topic and write notes on it. This is an enormous encouragement to students, since they are not thrown pen in hand onto a sheet
of white paper.

I once did this exercise with a remedial class of sixteen-year-olds
whose reading and writing skills were well below those of fifth graders
(ten-year-olds). The topic of truancy was, therefore, one close to their
hearts, and their scenarios revealed that. Warren's reason for cutting
school was to avoid a test. When his mother found out the truth, from
Warren himself, she was so afraid he would be suspended that she
made up an excuse for the teacher, thereby compounding Warren's
original lie. Another boy, Rodman, chose "going to a party" as his
reason. He lied to his parents, but told his teacher the truth. Rodman
decided his parents would never find out the truth. When I asked him
how he would stop them from finding out, he said that his teacher
would protect him: she would lie to his parents because she knew how
harsh they were to their own son. I then asked Rodman to write the
scene between the teacher and the boy, and then a scene between the
boy and the parents, illustrating the kind of harshness he had spoken
of. Rodman wrote more in that session than at any other that school
year.

Finally, my advice for encouraging students is basic to all writers:
use a notebook! I tell them to act like Harriet in *Harriet the Spy* (a
children's novel by Louise Fitzhugh) and save overheard snippets of
conversation, or just ideas that come into their heads, as material for
future plays. Note down simple things that seem a little odd. Good
places for spying are cafeterias, bus or train stops, offices, supermarkets,
trips to and from school . . . anywhere, really. A variation could be to
have your students spy in the same place every day for a week at the
same time. Warn them that they must never, *never* invade anyone's
privacy. Collect these examples of typical neighborhood conversation
and analyze the subject matter, style of language, type of jokes, and
so on, as well as the characters who habitually congregate in those
places. This will create a vivid picture of local life, its people, and its
voice.

Group Playwriting

Writing plays as a group requires careful planning, sometimes refer-
eeing, by the teachers. After all, some of your students are developing
their own sensibilities as writers, and. as pointed out earlier, may be
frustrated by having their individual impulses blocked. There are four

kinds of plays you might consider writing together: adaptations, original scenarios, plays about real events, and plays expressing a group identity (graffiti theatre).

Adaptations

Personally, I do not find it worth the time or trouble to involve a class in a dramatic adaptation of a novel or other classic source. There are already so many published versions that are quite well done that one might as well move students towards writing an original work. It is true there is a dearth of good material for school plays, but instead of resorting to adaptations, in which the kids might have little heartfelt investment, why not try getting them to write their own plays?

Original scenarios

This can be the most rewarding kind of group play for all involved, including the actors who might later perform in it.

When writing an original scenario as a group, you should act as a chairperson, helping to weld the different suggestions into a coherent structure as well as ensuring that everyone becomes fairly evenly involved. A striking example of a group-written play using an original scenario is *Thirteen Heavens and Nine Hells* (1988), written by a drama class at the Cambridge School of Weston, Massachusetts.

Field suggestions for a topic or develop one from improvisation. Fashion a story into several scenes—to get everyone involved, the number of scenes can equal the number of subgroups you create from the entire class. For instance, a thirty-five member class broken up into seven groups of five means seven scenes. Make notes for each scene on the blackboard. Agree on names for the main characters.

Remind the students that each scene must have a specific point to it and move the action forward, or allow a character time for reflection. Make sure that each scene's *where*, *who*, and *what* are specific.

Sometimes I wait until the end of this planning process before asking for volunteers to work out a particular scene; sometimes I get groups started on a scene as soon as it is roughed out. The first method allows everyone to know the direction of the whole story before they go into their groups, but it is a long, involved, time-consuming process. If you sense impatience in the class, rely on and trust the enthusiasm some of your students will feel for a particular scene that has just been roughed out, and let them get to work on it. At this stage, it will not matter that they do not know what everyone else is doing. It can be an advantage, since it encourages students to concentrate on their own scene, and not to try and preempt someone else's. This can also lead to some surprises and apparent contradictions which can make for a lively reading of the first draft of the play!

Try to make each group a judicious mix of the shy or weak writers and the more confident students.

This kind of group-writing process, involving the cooperation and collaboration of the whole class is hard, and the results, to begin with, may not be as original or interesting as some individually written plays. However, there are definite compensations. One of these is that this process encourages students to take more time and write longer scenes. Instead of writing small, episodic scenes that follow a character from situation to situation, they have to write one substantial scene as part of a group of other substantial scenes.

Another advantage, mentioned earlier, is the natural tendency toward inconsistencies between scenes, especially if the groups begin writing before they know the whole plot. These inconsistencies are not necessarily flaws. They can point out alternative possibilities for the plot, which perhaps had not been explored in the initial improvisations. They often make the plays more lifelike and interesting. Sometimes they need to be straightened out in subsequent drafts, but more often than not, they provide just the right surprise and need to be retained or only slightly revised for dramatic effect.

Yet another advantage to the group-writing process is that the promise of performance, if by the playwriting group itself, will stimulate the writers to give themselves good parts. I remember an incredibly involved plot that included a re-enactment of a battle in the American Revolution and was devised by some nine-year-olds in a Greenwich Village school. One boy, who was dyslexic, wrote out his section of this scene with great enthusiasm, albeit painfully slowly, because he wanted to act the main part of an embattled and heroic officer. On the appointed day, he arrived at school complete with home-made costume and toy rifle, having learned his part word-for-word.

Plays about real events

There are hundreds of variations for writing plays based on real events. The technical process is basically the same as described above. Here are some actual examples from workshops conducted in London.

1. Fictional Reconstructions ☐ This was similar to the Headlines exercise (see Chapter 2). A group of fifteen-year-olds in a London classroom discussed some ideas surrounding a recent murder. They knew nothing more than the brief report in the newspaper, so the play was not researched but invented as a fictional interpretation of the actual event. This allowed for some unusual points of view: they chose to follow the story of a little boy who is an innocent witness to the killing.

The murder scene was never written, but the scene after the murder, which follows, illustrates the improvisational quality of the dialogue and could well be a beginning for a longer piece.

SCENE 3. *Outside the fish-and-chips shop. There is a dead body on the floor.*

FITZROY: Oh shit!

MICKO: What you done now?

BORIS: I've told you to control your temper so many times, now look what you gone and done.

FITZROY: Tell me, did I mean it?

CHER: 'Course you didn't, darling. *(She offers him a drag)*

FITZROY: Thanks, doll, at least I know someone won't snitch.

CHER: Stupid idiot shouldn't've stuck his nose in anyway.

LUCY: We weren't going to hurt the little squirt anyway.

MICKO: Where is the little fucker?

MARY: Look, he is trying to slide off.

FITZROY: Come 'ere.

ERVISS: I'm coming.

MICKO: Move it, will yer.

ERVISS: I ain't bionic yer know.

FITZROY: Don't come it cheeky.

BORIS: I'm going, OK.

FITZROY: Mummy's boy.

LUCY: Mustn't be out later than eleven or he'll get his bottom smacked.

FITZROY: Scram, we don't want you hanging around here yer little poofta.

BORIS: Fuck off.

FITZROY: Better not blab or you'll be done in.

BORIS: As if I bleeding would.

MICKO: Course he won't. See yer.

CHER AND MARY: See yer kid.

LUCY: I'll follow on soon, alright lover. *(Boris goes)*

MARY: How many years'll you get.

FITZROY: You're great, fanks.

MARY: What yer mean, fanks.

FITZROY: Sounds as if you can't bleeding wait to get me into the nick.

MARY: You're bound to be caught ain't yer.

FITZROY: Oh God! Not unless someone blabs.

LUCY: I'm going.

FITZROY: Don't . . .

LUCY: I won't blab OK?!

FITZROY: Alright, have fun!

LUCY: You bet I will!

MICKO: What we gonna do wiv the brat.

FITZROY: He won't blab.

ERVISS: I'm scared they're gonna think it was me. *(He bursts into tears)*

FITZROY: Oh dear, innit a shame, the kid's going to get blood all over his hands. 'Ere, cop 'old o' this. *(Fitzroy shoves knife into Erviss's hands)* Let that add to your troubles.

MARY: Oh, you silly boy, now the kid's got his fingerprints all over the knife and you've got gloves on.

FITZROY: So I have.

(Kid runs off, yelling, drops knife)

ERVISS: I'm gonna tell the cops.

CHER: You bloody do and your family are gonna die wiv yer.

(Kid returns)

ERVISS: You better not do nothing to my family.

FITZROY: We won't unless . . .

ERVISS: I squeal?

FITZROY: Go on then, you're a good kid.

(Erviss goes)

MICKO: Well what you going to do wiv 'im?

LUCY: Why not leave a note on 'im saying "Accidents will 'appen" or summink like that.

FITZROY: Just leave 'im in the gutter.

LUCY: I'm leaving a note saying this is where all wogs belong.

FITZROY: Have you ever been nicked?

LUCY: Yeah, why?

FITZROY: Well you ain't leavin' no notes then.

MICKO: Why shouldn't she?

FITZROY: 'Cos they've got some record against her, see?

CHER: Oh, shame.

LUCY: Yeah.

FITZROY: Come on then, Cher, we're going.

CHER: See you lot at one outside church. *(Cher goes)*

LUCY: Of all places . . . OK see you.

MICKO: Let's scram.

MARY: I'm phoning the law.

MICKO: You what?

MARY: I'm phoning the cops. I ain't being lumbered with the thought of helping a murder, I'd prefer to be beaten up.

MICKO: OK but don't expect me to help you.

MARY: We'll have to go our separate ways if we can't stick together through this.

MICKO: Sorry kid, see you kid, good luck!

(Boy walks off. Girl goes into chip shop to use phone. Lucy goes off, Mary phones)

In the scene above, Lucy's line, "I'm leaving a note saying this is where all wogs belong" suggests a racial murder.

In December 1978, a black teenager, Michael Ferreira, was murdered by white youths in London. Early in 1979, a class of thirteen-year-olds at Langdon Park elementary school, in the East End of London, created their own play entitled *Who Killed Michael Ferreira?* It was a fiercely partisan play, accusing the police of unnecessary delay in allowing Michael to be taken to the hospital, thereby implicating them in his death. The scene that follows is markedly different from the previous piece. This one has a surface flatness, a starkness that communicates one particular point of view cleanly and without ambiguity.

SCENE 4. *Outside the Mortuary. Mr. and Mrs. Ferreira are waiting to see the body of their son.*

ATTENDANT: *(Opening the door)* I'm sorry, but you can't come in.

MR. FERREIRA: Look, we want to see our son's body, that's all.

ATTENDANT: Well, you can't come in. The coroner said that no one, only the police, can see the body yet.

MRS. FERREIRA: *(Passionately)* I want to see my son. . . . please let me see my son.

ATTENDANT: I'm sorry, madam, I can't let you in.

MRS. FERREIRA: I brought him into the world—now can't I see him now he's dead?

POLICEMAN 1: *(Entering)* Move along please, we don't want any more disturbances here.

MR. FERREIRA: You've got our son in there. We want to see him!

POLICEMAN 1: Well you can't, now move along home or I'll have to nick you for obstruction. *(He tries to take Mrs. Ferreira's arm)*

MRS. FERREIRA: Don't you touch me! You were the ones who killed my boy. You'll never hear the last of this.

POLICEMAN 1: You don't know what you're on about, you blacks are all the same.

MR. FERREIRA: You! Racist! Listen to me—we're going to get all our people together and we're going to fight your dirty racism! We're as much a part of this country as anyone.

MRS. FERREIRA: We'll make a movement to help all the black people, and we'll clear racism right off the streets of this country!

(The action freezes)

This script has no subtlety—deliberately so, since it was written as a passionate protest from a young, multiracial community to the authorities. The play was part of an explicitly antiracist pedagogy developed in the school by several teachers. They sought to introduce into the classroom the knowledge of certain social relationships, such as black and white solidarity as opposed to hostility, and of political power structures that are often kept hidden from school students because they must adhere to a conventional, establishment-oriented curriculum. Writing a play, remember, encourages empathy, and, therefore, an imaginative understanding of "alternative" points of view. Performing a play offers these points of view back to the community. For the pupils who asked the question Who killed Michael Ferreira? the answer was much more than the sum of their research or the excitement of performing something they had written; it was risking a commitment to a social and practical ideal, to a quest for justice. The irony is that their work was not only censored but ultimately banned by their own school. The play became hidden knowledge, disseminated surreptitiously like samizdat literature.

2. Living Newspapers and Plays About Issues ☐ Dramatizations of current affairs, such as court cases, are a very popular activity that can become part of a routine (perhaps weekly) that hones the writers' skills. Sometimes, as with the example above, a particular case may inspire an ambitious work, but often Living Newspapers can consist of short playlets that imitate the structure of news items on television.

These playlets can be both topical and controversial. A social studies teacher in New York used the notorious Bernhard Goetz case by quoting one of the youths Goetz shot: "Just because we all have criminal records, it doesn't mean that we're bad people."

This statement became the first line of an improvisation that argued the general assumptions behind the case as well as its specific pros and cons.

Some newspaper articles are wonderful springboards into writing, not so much *on* the subject of the article, but around it. A favorite trick of mine is to give people the first part of an in-depth article and ask them to write a scene inspired by it. This encourages them not to be too literal, and to treat the material as source for a play of their own, rather than the basis of a straightforward adaptation of a newspaper story.

Challenge your students with articles on topics that are alien to them. They then have to find an anchor for the topic in their own reality, and this will help them in their efforts to write convincingly by making scenes and plays real. Assignments like this can demonstrate to students the importance of research, of experiencing the unfamiliar, or of learning other people's languages.

3. Plays Expressing A Group Identity: Graffiti Theatre ☐ Sometimes, a particular group wants to communicate a message about itself. Some famous theatrical examples of this are *A Chorus Line, Runaways,*

and *For Colored Girls*. All these shows use monologues as their principal
dramatic device. They appeal to our natural curiosity about people
different from us—people who talk openly and candidly about themselves. They also demand that we listen carefully because, taken together, these monologues are like a patchwork quilt, representing a
collective statement about a way of life. That is why I call it graffiti
theatre—no other form comes so close to an identification between
author and subject.

This kind of play is popular among young people. We have already
seen how warm-up exercises based on students' autobiographies may
be fashioned into a play. The Walden Theatre in Louisville, Kentucky,
regularly mounts performances that initially grew out of monologues
young playwrights had written. (One of these presentations entitled
Glimpses, is available from Dramatic Publishing Company in Woodstock, Illinois.)

In the 1975 Young Writers Festival in London, there was a wonderful example of graffiti theatre by a group of five people aged eleven
to twenty from the West Indian Drama Group in Bristol. The director,
Angela Roddaway, taped improvisations, discussions, and interviews
with the five about their experiences in Jamaica and in England. They
were transcribed and fashioned into a play entitled *How Do You Clean
a Sunflower?* The characters' names are the same as the authors', and
everything in the play actually happened. Here is Panchita's story of
her leaving for England.

At night, last thing, we used to go to Great Grandma's room. We'd all
gather there and say prayers and sing hymns and tell ghost stories. Great
Grandma's room had French windows leading onto the verandah. Her
sewing machine was by the window.
  Before that, in the evening, we used to go to the kitchen. It was a
separate building and it's the biggest kitchen you ever saw. We used to go
there to listen to reggae and dance and look after the pig food cooking
for the morning. There was everything in that pig food, bananas, yams,
everything. It would cool down during the night and be all nice for the hogs
in the morning.
  Sometimes, at night, we'd climb the pear tree. This was a tree on a
piece of high ground, and the tree had once been struck by lightning but it
still bears. When you climb the tree you can see right over to Garland.
We used to watch the big events there when we weren't allowed to go.
  There was a valley where we played cricket. All the way to the cross
roads was our dad's land, so big you could get lost. Cane, then bananas.
  And there was fresh spring water and wild berries and the food was
good and rich, fresh, not frozen.
  When we came here, the first thing I did was go out in the yard, and
the only flower there was a sunflower. It was covered with soot and smuts
from the railway and I thought, "How do you clean a sunflower?"

Notice how very verbal this is. Given the inexperience of the writer,
and the tendency of young writers to censor themselves on paper, it

is unlikely this passage would have been as moving, as immediate, had it not been caught in the speaker's voice and only then set down on paper.

Something else that really happened was eighteen-year-old Alfred's decision to marry his pregnant white girlfriend, Rosemary. In one scene, Panchita refers patronizingly to the unborn child, and Alfred explodes:

ALFRED: What do you mean—"poor little thing"? Why do you keep saying
    "poor little thing"? I'm fed up with it. Don't you let me hear you
    say that again. My kid's gonna have the best. The best of everything.
    Nobody's going to take it out on him—or her—whatever it is. Whatever
    it's gonna be, I'm gonna make it the best. Yeah, if we're not accepted
    I'm gonna make us accepted, and I don't want to hear you nor anybody
    else say anything like that about my child again.

PANCHITA: (Stunned) What?

ALFRED: "Poor little thing." What did you mean by it, "poor little thing"?
    There's lots more poor than her—or him. (Panchita gets up and stands
    right, facing away from him) That's right! Take a look. Take a look out in
    the streets. Do you see any poor out there? 'Cos if you do you can
    know my kid ain't gonna be like that. I don't know whether it's gonna
    be her or him so I have to say "it" but I'm gonna make sure it won't
    need no pity. You digging? OK. Get wise, you know, 'cos I'm gonna say
    it again. "My kid ain't gonna be no poor little thing." OK. Forget it!
    Just this once I'm gonna forget it but don't make the same mistake
    again, OK? Else I'm just gonna go right offa my head.

ANDREW: You already have.

PANCHITA: I only meant that anything that's born into this world comes
    little and poor.

In another scene, Alfred arrives late for the wedding reception, because on the way back from the church Rosemary went into labor, and he had to take her to the hospital. A half-page after that scene, the play ends—with the arrival of Alfred and Rosemary's child, there was no more time for scripting sessions. Rehearsals began, but two weeks before the first Bristol performance, Alfred and Rosemary's "golden baby" died. The play was temporarily abandoned, frozen into forty-six tattered pages of typescript. That November, it came to life in the Theatre Upstairs at the Royal Court, and Alfred, Rosemary, Charles, and Elaine came with it and performed it themselves. Their play told a particular story, at a particular time and place in their lives.

As your groups work on their plays, even those who at first are most reluctant to give up the creative freedom of individual writing will recognize and appreciate the challenge of working in tandem with others—and this, in turn, will be a good introduction for the apprentice playwright to the teamwork necessary for play production. That is, after all, the ultimate goal of playwriting.

6

□□□□□□□□□□□□□□□□□□
□□□□□□□□□□□□□□□□□□

The Form of
Playwriting

■■■■■■■■■■■■■■■■■■■■

In chapter 1 we looked at the elements that a group of sixth graders said make for a good play. Those elements were part of that class's shared language, their own agreed-upon terms. The elements of drama, as defined by Aristotle in *The Poetics*, are Plot, Character, Thought, Diction, Music, and Spectacle. If we decode what the students were actually saying, we will find that they had, without benefit of instruction, discovered the importance of these six elements! "A play must grab the audience's attention, so they can relate to and be involved with it"—what these students were groping for were the concepts of Plot and Character. "Plays must be real"—it is the diction the playwright chooses to use in his or her play which helps to make the chosen situation, no matter how outlandish, absolutely real to the audience. "Plays should not be racist," "The message must be clear"—Thought is variously defined as a play's subject, theme, or message. These sixth graders were using a narrow definition. To them, the most important message was that a play must never be racist. As was demonstrated by *Reggae Brittania* (see chapter 3), a play can present a racist character in order to denigrate racism. "Plays are visual, not just words"—Spectacle. It is fascinating to see how students, when asked to think about what they look for in a play, are unconsciously on target, even if their terms of reference are localized to their personal experiences.

"All" that remains to be done is to help the apprentice playwrights form these diverse elements into a play. How do we take all the elements we have looked at—how to develop scenes and characters, and what to look for when creating dialogue—and shape them into a play?

We have looked at how to go about writing, rewriting, and structuring scenes. But the perfect scene is not the raison d'etre for playwriting; it is a step to creating a play. Everything we have discussed about constructing a scene applies to the construction of a play. Let us look now at how to make a play.

Plays are based on conflict—between perceptions, ideas, individuals. Characters have goals and desires, defined as objectives in our improvisation exercises, and each character is going to pursue his or her own goal. The playwright must give equal weight to each opposing desire or viewpoint. This creates the conflict.

Real drama lies in the change arising from the conflict, and in the choices made. We said earlier that in a situation of conflict, the characters must make choices, and each choice costs something. Choices made can lead to further conflict, and to further change. This is the core of a play. Not the heart; the emotional impetus lies in the characters.

Basic Play Structure, in Five Parts

There is the conventional format for structuring a play. Obviously, there are many plays in the world's literature that ignore this format and create their own, but this is almost always done by experienced playwrights who have mastered the conventional form first. It is worth recalling that e.e. cummings, that so often cited "rebel" of the poetic form, first mastered the forms of meter and verse before his great experiment with (or without) punctuation and conventional orthography. Less well known is that toward the end of his career, he returned to more conventional forms. Challenge is found in structure and freedom, as well: if you master the form, you can concentrate on content. And then you can play with form.

The basic format for a play's structure is as follows:

1. Background/basic situation.
2. Rising action, initial complications.
3. Climax.
4. Falling action; fewer complications; a resolve that leads toward the denouement.
5. Denouement and conclusion.

No play (no good play) in history has ever followed this pattern slavishly.

We can see that a play is not a simple up-and-down structure. Without frightening off young playwrights, let's complicate the basic structure a bit by paring it down to the beginning, the middle, and the end.

The opening of a play, the beginning, establishes the basic situation and the characters. It will also serve to establish our initial sympathies—which may soon be upset, within the space of the same scene that establishes them. Claudius, in his first speech, seems very rational, a good king, an affectionate husband and uncle. Our opinion of him is soon changed because our sympathies lie with Hamlet—we must accept his point of view.

The next step in the beginning section of a play introduces the elements that will upset the basic situation. This will be the basic complication of the play, the one that motivates the rest of the plot.

You have established the basic conflict. Now you can turn it back on itself, complicate the conflict further. A complication is something that comes between the protagonist and his goal. Take the child in the Gasman Cometh improv. The child's goal was simply to get something to eat. First, the argument between the parents blocked his achievement of that goal, and then, more drastically, the arrival of the gasman who will turn off the gas and the stove. There you have two complications leading up to the height of the action. In a play based on the Green People improv, you could start with the green character on stage who seems perfectly normal. The other character, the one who is seeing people turn green, enters, and upsets that basic assumption. It also serves to upset Green's complacency that his alien plot is going along perfectly smoothly—A has seen people turning green! A knows! This is a perfectly reasonable complication. Now, why is A seeing people turning green while other people apparently are not?

The point of the rising action of a play is to establish the conflicts and complicate the basic situation as much as possible. Nonstop conflict and complications, like the nonstop car chases of television shows, dull the interest and concentration of the audience. A playwright plays with his or her audience as an angler plays with a fish—play it along, ease up on the tension only to increase it further as the play progresses. The major complications occur before the climax of a play—but not all of them. It is misleading to speak of "the" climax. All conflict and complications are and have little climaxes, a point at which a change or choice is made, that will end that complication, but which may well lead to the next one, whether immediately or a scene or two down the line. You cannot have the primary climax square in the middle of a play, as is suggested by the basic outline above. After the climax, tension decreases. All decisions have been made. There can be no further complications or changes. The climax is the ultimate change. However, there is a point in a play when all the complications thrown in the way of the protagonist come to a head, when a certain course of action becomes irrevocable. For instance, in *Hamlet*, this point is the end of the Play scene, when Hamlet knows for certain that the Ghost spoke the truth about his father's murder—and when Claudius is certain that Hamlet knows of his guilt. It is a two-fold climax, and the second part is as important as the first. It is the basis for the complications in the rest of the play—Claudius's attempt to have Hamlet killed in England, Hamlet's thwarting of those plans. The deaths of Polonius and then Ophelia further complicate the action and are further climaxes. Without them, Claudius would not have been able to use Laertes as his tool to be rid of Hamlet. The ultimate climax of the play is, of course, the death of Hamlet, when all is revealed and resolved.

Resolution/Earning the Resolution

We saw in the structuring of scenes that events cannot come out of thin air. Everything in a play must build on what has gone before, and that applies to the resolution. Frequently seen in young people's writing are plays full of abuse, drunkenness, and violence—and the plays end happily, speedily. The play simply lurches into a cozy and comforting finale, usually with the words, "I forgive you":

FATHER: From now on, I promise I will never hit you again.

AMY: And please don't drink anymore.

FATHER: I will not drink anymore.

(Amy and her father never ever had no more quarrels and she and her father are the best of friends.)

Endings of this sort are rarely earned; that is, set up by events earlier in the play. More often than not, the drunken and abusive father comes to his senses at the first sign of trouble.

Resolutions end the conflict, one way or another, whether the protagonist wins or loses, lives or dies. Some may suggest that all that has been wrong will be righted; but the possibility of this happening has been strongly established earlier in the play. If all the actions in a play point to a comfortable resolution, one with the protagonist winning through, it is not drama to throw it all over suddenly with death and destruction. It is cheap and unearned. Nor can a play which looks to end with the destruction of the protagonist suddenly and without warning become land of hope and glory. The deus ex machina is not an acceptable stage device. Audiences expect to be treated better.

Young playwrights have already become familiar with, and possibly proficient in, the idea of fighting for the right to remain on stage. They know that a character must have a reason to be on stage—otherwise, what is he or she doing there? Resolutions of plays should be looked at in the same way: there must be reason for everything that happens in a play, including the resolution. Anything else is unsatisfactory for the audience, and probably, ultimately, for the playwright.

Back in chapter 2, when we looked at finding the true drama behind a "dramatic" moment, we worked backward from the climax. Playwrights usually have their eye firmly fixed on the climax they wish to achieve while they work on the rest of the play. This can be achieved through asking pertinent questions, one of the strongest being *why*. What is Green's plot, and *why*? The established conflict here is likely to be A vs. Green, Green determined to carry out his verdant plot, A determined to stop him. A can be viewed as the protagonist, Green as the antagonist. A's goal is to prevent the world from being turned green. Green's goal is to see that it is. Green is the antagonist.

Let's look now at the role of character in a play. Obviously, character is the bearer of the plot. Plot is defined as character in action. Plot and Character are also the first two of Aristotle's elements of drama. The characters are usually designed and created to fit the plot. Working the other way around sometimes succeeds, but only if the plot is motivated exclusively by the life and conflicts of that character (viz., *The Heidi Chronicles*).

Antagonist is a term we have not discussed before, except very obliquely when we spoke of points of view and being fair to each character. An antagonist is not necessarily a villain. The antagonist can be viewed as the personification of the obstacles in the path of the protagonist. There need not be a single antagonist, but the effect of the antagonist must be as strong as the striving of the protagonist after his or her goal. It must also be portrayed as fairly and realistically as the protagonist. Remember, in order to manipulate points of view and thereby audience reaction, every character must be real and valid. The audience must believe in them all as human beings. It does not serve the message of the play to have the protagonist opposed by cardboard figures mouthing a despised viewpoint.

There are several fine books on the actual structuring of plays—some of these are listed in the bibliography. All of them go into great depth on all aspects of putting a play together. Encourage young playwrights who are joyously discovering their craft to seek out these books and read them for the sheer pleasure they give. An especially fine example is Louis Catron's *Writing, Producing, and Selling Your Play*

(1984), a no-nonsense look at both the artistic and practical side of playwriting.

Here is a list of guidelines to use when working with playwrights:

1. Know what *your* goal as a playwright is. Establish in your mind what your climax is to be, and keep that in mind at all times. Write it down where you can see it while you're writing.
2. Decide what you want to say, what the message is, in your play. This is the theme.
3. Decide how you will present it. This is the plot.
4. Develop the bearers of the plot—your characters.
5. Make your characters real. Ensure that they speak as real people do. This does not mean a play consists of meaningless, casual exchanges in the interests of "reality." A play must be unreality anchored in realism. This includes taking particular notice of how characters speak, making sure they don't all sound alike. (This is a version of Aristotle's Diction.)
6. Remember that each scene in a play is a little play—it must be complete in itself. It must involve the goal of the protagonist. If a scene does not move the action forward in some way, it should go—no matter how exquisitely written! This is one of the hardest lessons for any writer in any medium to learn.
7. Remember that each character, especially the protagonist, must be motivated in everything he or she does. Do not clutter your scenes with characters who have no purpose. If they do not help advance the action, get rid of them.
8. If the climax of the play is the resolution, remember that a secondary climax usually occurs after the basic situation has been explored and complicated by events and people. This is the ultimate complication to the conflict and can be an action that starts hurtling toward the point at which is it rendered inevitable.
9. Loose ends must be tied up at the resolution. If the action of the play has not sufficiently explained everything, a last-minute speech is not going to.

Playwriting does not end with "Curtain." There is always rewriting to be done . . . . and in playwriting, this is not a private process but one that is almost brutally public. It makes the earlier experiences of the improvisation drafts useful in readying young playwrights for revision and rewriting—and for the ultimate performance. We will now look at methods of encouraging rewriting and revision.

7

Evaluating and Rewriting

Before students begin their first draft, I always tell them, "Don't censor yourselves. Remember, this is only a first draft." Despite this advice, of course, there are always those who block themselves immediately, the internal censor being very strong, or who repeatedly write the first few lines, scrap them, and begin again. It is as if the prospect of rewriting is simply too horrible or too embarrassing to contemplate. Writers sabotage their initial instincts by feeling they must achieve a perfect draft the first time; it is an almost insurmountable obstacle. They deny themselves the unfettered energy on which instinct relies.

Rewriting is a central fact of playwriting, right up to the first night and even beyond. Simon Gray rewrote his play *The Common Pursuit* for the United States premiere because he had been unsatisfied with the British production, and even Neil Simon has rewritten his hit play *The Odd Couple*. This section looks at several examples of the most common errors that young playwrights make, and a few simple keys to guiding their rewriting.

As a starting point, here is the checklist the New York Young Playwrights Festival used from 1983 to 1985. This was used as a guide for the judges when compiling their evaluations of the entries. This list of comments touches on the most common problems that recur in the work of young playwrights; problems in creating believable dialogue, well-defined characters, plots that involve the audience, and honest, credible, dramatic action. Anyone evaluating the work of apprentice playwrights can use these numbered comments to analyze a student's draft.

CHARACTERIZATION

1. For us to care about your characters and about what happens to
   them, we need to get to know them better. You can do this
   by developing your scenes and making them longer so that we
   spend more time with the people in them.
2. We need more information about your characters. You cannot
   assume that the audience knows anything about your characters
   except what they see them do, hear them say, or hear other
   characters say about them on stage.
3. Your characters lack dimension and so are difficult for us to
   believe in. Let's see your characters in different situations. To see
   someone from a constant single point of view simplifies that
   person and tends to push him or her toward a stereotype. The
   audience needs to be able to understand and identify with all
   the characters and their opposing needs and points of view.

DIALOGUE

4. Your characters tend to sound the same. Try to liven up the
   dialogue by giving each character a particular "voice"—his or her
   own way of talking to people. Listen to people talking and try
   to capture the reality of their conversations in dialogue form.
   Remember that people also change the way they speak according
   to the situation they are in.

NARRATIVE

5. Drama does not necessarily consist of a string of exciting
   incidents. What makes us interested in a plot is often *why*
   something happens, not just what happens. In this way, we can
   get more involved in the plot and feel something for the
   characters instead of merely remaining observers. You can excite
   an audience with suspense, holding the action back for a while.
   Or you can show the characters wrestling with a problem, trying
   to resolve a conflict.
6. Be careful to research your material thoroughly so that your play
   convinces us. Otherwise, audiences may not take your play
   seriously.
7. You have a good imagination. You might try next to write a play
   about people and problems that you know well. Then you could
   use your imagination to supply details of characters' behavior
   that will make them real to an audience.
8. To get involved in a play, the audience must be able to follow
   the story and believe in it. The more extreme the action, the more
   important it is to provide details that will convince the audience
   of its reality.

9. A play tells a story through dialogue and dramatic action. Instead of using a narrator (which is a storytelling technique), try to dramatize the story by showing us what happens and what people say to each other.

Of course, it is one thing to be able to pinpoint the shortcomings in students' work, but how can they be guided to analyze their own writing and make decisions on how best to revise? The following section outlines some ways to encourage evaluation and rewriting in the classroom.

Expansion and Economy

Apprentice playwrights usually need to expand their work in a second draft—rarely is it cutting that is needed. More confident students' work will occasionally become prolix, even in a first draft—these students are usually the stars of a creative writing course and have written a one-hundred page novel (by the age of thirteen) and need to learn to underwrite.

The key is to tell the young playwright not to panic. Do not be afraid of spending time on a scene. Sometimes this is hard, since the brain does race along so much more quickly than the hand can follow. Playwrights become frustrated, impatient, and so spend less time on a situation or plot development than they ought. Paradoxically, it is hard for young playwrights to learn true economy in dialogue until they have experienced the falseness of overwriting. My advice, then, is to urge your students to err on the side of overwriting. Let them develop the scenes and characters and make themes explicit. Then they can see what they have before they begin to pare it all down.

Voice

Dialogue must correspond in some way to a human voice. We must understand that "the human voice underlies the entire writing process, and shows itself throughout the life of the writer." (Graves 1983). And, "writing floats on a sea of speech" (Britton, in Graves 1983), a metaphor that helps us gauge a common error in first drafts: literariness. Reading plays aloud, or, preferably, acting them, helps the writers hear mistakes they might not see.

A version of literary writing that is especially pernicious is that in which a writer tries to show off his or her cleverness. This kind of self-consciousness is best cured by an observation exercise, whether it be around the school, in the neighborhood, or even at home, and by transcribing the spontaneous results.

As well as relating to the characters' dialogue, voice ultimately relates to the individuality of the writer's work as a whole—its personality, its style. Some young playwrights do not risk revealing those things that make them different from other people. Sometimes their work is too personal and private, so that what they are trying to say cannot be heard.

Theme and Focus

Some themes are too large and unwieldy. The writer cannot control them or becomes bored when his or her grand idea seems thin on paper. The writer needs to be more selective, needs to home in on the one action that contains the richest potential for conflict that leads to transformation. Usually this is right before or just after the climactic scene. Students need to learn how to linger in the present, rather than rush on to the next incident. The lingering can foreshadow, even rehearse the coming scenes. Think of Hamlet planning what he wants to do.

By focussing in detail on the minimum rather than maximum number of incidents, young playwrights learn to write in a more sustained way; they experiment with scenes of continuous action rather than numerous smaller fragments. Writing like this will also clarify what the play is about, for the writer as well as the audience, and will spur the play through unnecessary exposition to the central dramatic action.

Realism

Stereotypical characters or copies of TV shows and movies will continue to satisfy the class only if the teacher fails to challenge them. When analyzing improvisations as well as responding to a shared first draft, test the work not so much against people's personal taste but against the more objective yardstick of people's awareness of social reality. Balance opposing viewpoints about character or situation so that they build complexity into each. Test for a writer's personal investment. A good question to ask is, Is this merely imitation, or is this a topic that has been generated from fresh thinking and firsthand emotions—and will it generate more?

Emphasize research as a way of furnishing detail that will anchor the play in a believable reality. This is just as true about dream/fantasy/ghost plays as it is about more naturalistic work. In fact, the more extreme or fantastic the play the more important it is to provide details with which to engage an audience, to suspend their disbelief, or compel their attention while they remain aloof or skeptical.

Evaluation in the Classroom

The main technique for evaluating students' first drafts in the classroom is the script conference, which may be held in small peer groups of two to six people, one-on-one conferences between teacher and student, or together as the whole class. Here are some specific approaches to take in responding to work.

Modeling the Evaluation

Just as I model a script's layout by writing out the first few moments of a scene on the blackboard, I model a way for the students to think about and criticize their own and one another's work by sharing a few people's plays with the whole group, and taking the lead in asking certain types of questions. The questions are similar to ones I have asked these writers privately while they were still writing.

- ☐ How do you feel about it?
- ☐ What's going to happen next?
- ☐ Did you have any false starts?
- ☐ Did you plan it out in advance, or was it a stream?
- ☐ What was your starter? What made you choose to write the first few lines the way you did?
- ☐ What problems did you have?
- ☐ Did you solve them satisfactorily?
- ☐ What problems do you feel remain?
- ☐ What's the main thing you're trying to say?
- ☐ What's your favorite bit?

These questions are about content and process. I complement them with comments about the situation and characters, and I ask for clarification if necessary. The questions, however, usually provide the answers.

Whole Class Evaluation

I usually ask students to read out their own first drafts. Someone else's reading it inevitably turns into a performance, and it is usually too early for that. Students also can read their own writing better—they can fill in missing words and give clues to the tone of the piece.

The next set of questions is for the class to consider.

- ☐ What did you like about this play?
- ☐ What did you feel about the characters?
- ☐ Did you have a gut reaction to the piece?

☐ What sort of emotion is the play provoking?

☐ How did the play do this? What lines of dialogue or situations really hit home to you as an audience?

☐ Did the dialogue flow? Could you believe it?

☐ Were the characters interesting? What made them so?

☐ What did the characters want of each other?

☐ What did they do to get what they wanted? Did they succeed?

☐ Who do you think is the main character (protagonist)?

☐ Is there a conflict?

☐ Where does it lead? Is there a point of transformation? What is that point?

☐ Does the scene need more detail?

☐ What could happen next?

☐ Did anything confuse you?

☐ What suggestions do you have for the writer to consider incorporating into the second draft?

None of these questions invites negative, destructive criticism. They demand as much of the class offering the criticism as they demand of the playwright. You will notice that these questions are similar to the ones used in analyzing an improvisation—they will be familiar to the students who will already have some experience in receiving and offering criticism in a mutually supportive manner. Analyzing the draft improvisations prepares the students to analyze a more completely written work. Gradually, the students will learn to rehearse these questions themselves and internalize them so that they need no longer rely just on an outsider's sympathetic response. They will reach the point at which they will be satisfied with their work, and only then offer it for outside comment.

Small Group Evaluation

I used to spend a long session listening to scene after scene, and I would try to galvanize the class—and myself—to comment. This is just too exhausting. I suggest modeling questions for up to four pieces at the most and then shift the initiative back to the students by putting them into small groups of three to six. It is up to them to question one another. The writers will learn to anticipate the questions and fill in the details long before the draft reaches the point of being read to the group. But this happens only if the same questions are being asked. Students rely on a pattern or routine of analysis and criticism, which you should try to offer them. It will help them develop a critical vocabulary—they'll learn how to use such words as "protagonist," "transformation," "tone," and "gesture." One way of reinforcing this is to move from verbal sharing of scripts to written responses—not so much reviews as an exchange of letters about one another's work.

As a guide to analysis, I'll offer you a few of the most common flaws in young playwrights' work, some examples, and then some ways of correcting these flaws.

Overreliance on the Visual □ Some plays are films in disguise that rely on a minimum of dialogue and a maximum of visual signs as a way of identifying characters. Or they are sidestepping the matter of true characterization by mere description. Here is an example from a student's dramatis personae:

BETH: Long brown hair, brown eyes, a pretty face and perfect posture. She is an A student going into the eleventh grade, and hangs around with a good bunch of kids. Beth is also on the swim team.

SUE: Beth's sister. She has short blond hair, blue eyes, and a pretty face. She is in the fifth grade and none of her friends live near her.

MOM: Beth's mom has short brown hair, brown eyes and is very trim looking. She is semi-strict and does not work but is involved in many activities.

And so on.

Analysis for Revision   Looks certainly do play an important part of our first impressions of people—but they are not how we get to know someone. While we have already seen the limitations of describing people by adjectives pertaining to their personality, in this case that is a place to start. Suggest to the student that one character trait, rather than a physical description, can mean many things in many different situations. Beth sounds as if she is an achiever—perhaps an overachiever?

Questions for the student to use in his or her own analysis:

□ Knowing these physical characteristics, do I really know this person?
□ What could these characteristics suggest about the person?
□ What is there that Beth could want, if she has such an enviable social position in the class?
□ If none of Sue's friends live nearby, how does this make Sue feel?
□ Mom is semi-strict. How, precisely, to show this? Why is she only semi-strict? Because it's the way parents are supposed to be, or has she learned she can afford to be with her children?

Urge the student to get to know the characters better, so that the audience can. And not to rely on physical descriptions only—if nothing else, it will certainly limit casting possibilities!

The next example is clearly a film.

SARAH: You know, next summer I may not be working here again. I wish
you were mine. I often dream about some miracle happening, that
would make you mine, forever. I only wish my dreams could come true.
*(A soft neighing comes from Charlenn. Sarah strokes the horse,
thoughtfully, as she gazes at the ducks swimming on the lake)* Well, I guess
we better get back. I've got a lot of work to get done! *(Sarah mounts
Charlenn and begins the journey back. As they pass through bushes and
trees, Charlenn jumps and prances nervously)* Whoa, Charlenn. Easy now,
girl. What on earth is wrong with you? You've been on this trail a
million times and you've never acted this jumpy. *(Places hand on Charlenn's neck)* What is it, girl? What's wrong? *(Charlenn jumps as a bird
flies from a nearby bush. Sarah becomes annoyed)* Now Charlenn you stop
that this minute. You're acting like a two-year-old! *(Sarah notices that
the horse is extremely nervous and jittery. She dismounts)* Okay, Charlenn.
I'll walk you back. Just relax, girl. It's okay. That was just an ol' bird.
It isn't gonna hurt you.

The horse is an important character in this scene. We need to see
its emotional reactions, its disturbance, not just Sarah's responses to
them, and the stage directions make it quite clear that this should be
a film. Suggest that the student work on a scene, perhaps using Sarah
and another character, that allows Sarah to interact in a human relationship. All the dynamics should be allowed to come into play.

Unearned Wish Fulfillment □ One of the strongest tendencies in
young playwrights' work is wish fulfillment, a modern variation on
the "and they all lived happily ever after." For example:

GREG: I'm sorry I left you and the baby. I see now how selfish I was. I'll
get a job, and you can go back to school. Will you forgive me?
NATALIE: I love you, Greg—of course I forgive you.

The key word to remember when talking to students about wish
fulfillment is *comforting*. This kind of sentimentality is pure comic-book
romance: the orphan magically finds her foster parents at Christmas,
the boy who has abandoned his pregnant girlfriend sees the baby and
returns. These writers have to realize that reconciliations and happiness, especially after such turmoil, have to be earned. People do indeed
change their behavior, but this change has to be fully accounted for
and dramatized.

QUESTIONS FOR ANALYSIS

□ What was the central dramatic action of the play? What brought
the matter of Greg's wandering to a crisis?
□ Is this resolution on his part true to anything we have seen in
the character before?

☐ If the character of Greg is to make this kind of a turnaround, did we see the potential for it earlier in the play? Always be true to your characters.

Moralizing ☐ Similar to the above is the tendency to moralize, and it, too, usually appears at the end of a script. In the following example, the erring husband returns to his wife and begs for her forgiveness. She replies:

Why should I? You're just a cad and your zipper stays down more than it stays up and you are very bad husband material. But I once loved you, but I want a divorce and I never want to see you again.
   (Ralph was the kind of man that lived on a woman's money, so he had no money, no wife, nowhere to go, so he kept on looking for someone. By the end of that year he was married to several women and divorced, and he became a lonely gigolo. That poor man. That's what you get when your zipper stays down more than it stays up.)

This play was like a soap opera, a never-ending saga of infidelity. The moral tag about the zipper (which sounds funny to adults but was meant very seriously by the twelve-year-old girl who wrote it), tacked on at the end of a ten-page script, drew this saga to a close. It has nothing to do with the reality of the final scene. It is sheer rhetoric, and its effect is to diminish the characters and make them puppets rather than real people.

Analysis for Revision   There is some very real drama implied within the final description; at least it traces the progress of a character. You should perhaps look at the final breakup of Ralph and his wife as the central dramatic action. Use that as the event that impels the play.

Building Trust

Building trust among the students, as well as between the students and you, the teacher, is vital to encouraging young playwrights to internalize the pattern of questioning. A teacher must insist on respect and good, intent listening. As the students feel less threatened by their peers, they will gain in confidence. This change in self-perception will probably be reflected in a change in topic choice. Encourage this—give students independence in selecting what they want to write about. Try to build a constant list of questions—don't spring surprises on them. Ask them to suggest additional questions for the list.

   However, the best resource for playwrights by far is not this checklist of questions, but the inspiration of listening to one another's work.

The methods described above treat the students seriously as dramatists who have something important to say. Attending to each person's scene becomes a fascinating source of other ideas, alternative ways of treating familiar subjects, and, more particularly, ways of treating unfamiliar, special, or taboo subjects.

The stimulus of listening to other people's plays helps a writer gain control over his or her own work. It actually provides a sense of craft, as well as a yardstick against which to judge one's own work. This becomes most useful when young playwrights get stuck. You can suggest to them some of the solutions that others in the class have discovered, or you can suggest that they scan their own previous work for inspiration. Writing a play thus becomes part of the class's, and the individual student's, writing tradition, rather than a single assignment that causes panic on all fronts. Eventually, students will begin to help one another without a teacher's prompting. When this happens, you will know that students have begun to understand what it requires to be a good playwright and a good audience.

Teaching Playwriting and Writing

Instinct is infallible. If it leads us astray, it is no longer instinct.
Igor Stravinsky, *Poetics of Music*

The previous chapters have dealt with the practice of playwriting and the risks students take when they first investigate this strange new form of communication.

The next chapters look at the pitfalls facing the teachers who are willing to take the risks alongside their students, and will, I hope, help them avoid some of the most common misconceptions in the theory of teaching playwriting.

The first lesson in writing is the same as the first lesson in playwriting: trust your instincts. They may provide an overall concept or a topic, or they may provide an image, an action, or a bit of conversation. Instinct does not necessarily indicate the easiest way to proceed. It may be too vague, and you may have to grope and experiment—brainstorm—before you are able to write anything.

The first impulse is very precious. It may be a modest start, but at this point, it is all your students, or indeed any writers, have to rely on. From this point, the process of writing and re-writing will be a laborious and complicated battle to connect that impulse to something on the paper. It can be disheartening. It involves many disciplines, some of which have nothing to do with actual writing skills. It is worth knowing factors such as the time available for your students to write, both in school and at home. But fundamentally, it is worth knowing that however reluctant or put off or discouraged a student may be, the instinct to inscribe one's existence in some way is immensely strong. Donald Graves's inspirational book, *Writing: Teachers and Children At Work* (1983, 3), begins with this paragraph:

> Children want to write. They want to write the first day they attend school. This is no accident. Before they went to school they marked up walls, pavements, newspapers with crayons, chalk, pens or pencils . . . anything that makes a mark. The child's marks say "I am."

This chapter looks at some ways of exploiting Graves' stirring optimism, and offers some general principles.

Time

Allow time in *each lesson* to write so that writing becomes habitual. It should be part of a routine of discussion, improvisation, writing, sharing, analysis, and rewriting.

This routine has variety, but it also has predictability, which will help create confidence and discipline. A set routine for playwriting lessons that includes ancillary matters such as pencil sharpening and collecting folders as well as problems like writer's block, will help those pupils who, in Graves's words, "meet themselves on the blank page" (92) and find no one there feel part of the overall activity, rather than feeling isolated, weak, or ignorant. A routine also encourages students to prepare for their writing by thinking about it at other times. Perhaps they make notes of ideas or overheard conversations. They bring these notes to the lesson, knowing that the notes are the material for playwriting, and that they are going about their craft in the same way as the professionals go about it.

This process helps students widen their choice of subject matter and develop their themes more effectively. It stimulates them to rewrite because they no longer feel pressured to finish something in one class period. They are no longer afraid to look back and see that their draft is not all they wanted or all it could be.

All these things help in the establishment of the second principle: ownership.

Ownership

A student who writes something merely for the teacher to mark with red ink has no sense of ownership, or power. A student who writes something just for his or her folder is equally isolated. Students frequently don't like the idea of writing because they do not know why they are doing it. They have no sense of their audience. And since they have no pride in their work, the writing becomes just another chore for school. This is reinforced by too early an insistence on grammar and spelling, which the students may misinterpret as a teacher's indifference to the content of the piece. A student's sense of ownership is diminished even more when the teacher corrects the work by literally taking it out of the student's hands.

Another common error for teachers is to focus too quickly on what a script lacks. Comment on what is present in the writing and respond to the achievement rather than the failings of the writer.

Nothing enhances a student's sense of ownership more than a teacher's writing his or her script along with the class: the teacher becomes a role model. You demand silence and concentration for at least five minutes while everyone, including you, starts writing. Share your script; ask for the students' response, discuss the problems you faced and the choices that you made. This helps remove the myth that adults write easily and fluently, that it is some kind of magic. You demonstrate that you understand the difficulties and that you are, in fact, learning with the class. This can be a scary move for a teacher to make, but it is also essential. It is the move from being the one who teaches to the one who does. The students, too, are being asked to take some pretty scary steps, to reveal themselves in their writing, and to hold that writing up to their peers.

Professional writers who work in schools should also demystify their work. In our school workshops for the Young Playwrights Festival, the professionals show, in person, what it is like to be a writer by talking about all aspects of their work. I remember some Brooklyn junior high school students gasping when Arthur Laurents told them that he had written *West Side Story*, but they were even more impressed when he took their apprentice works seriously and did not condescend in any way. Donald Graves recounts the story of Tolstoy being asked by some children to write for them a story about a boy who steals. He began composing while his students gathered around his desk. But instead of being awed by this great writer, the children quickly pointed out a mistake in Tolstoy's portrayal of the young thief. In his journal, Tolstoy later wrote that they were right to correct him, and he crystallized his views about this in an essay entitled "Are We To Teach the Peasant Children to Write, or Are They To Teach Us?"

This story powerfully reminds us that children know some subjects much better than we do. Their expertise is often hidden from us, but if we want to encourage ownership of their writing, we need to validate such expert knowledge as suitable, even ideal, topic choices. The most obvious areas are their home and street lives: the things that are precious or private to them including their political, social, or religious values; their heroes and heroines; the songs they sing while they play; their hobbies; their fears. Again, it is up to the teacher to model this kind of selection of subject matter by sharing, writing, and dramatizing certain personal experiences with the students. If this is done with care, it need not be at all embarrassing; and it gradually builds trust, respect, and ownership into the writing process.

Treating your students' plays seriously as drama means that you should use the same terms of reference as when you and the class study or perform adult dramatic literature. It will help students become more assertive in their analysis of their own work and of the professionals'. It will help them practice a critical process and the vocabulary that accompanies it, which will become the first step in revising and rewriting. This process then becomes part of the routine of playwriting, so that students begin to rely on their own judgment of their work as well as on others'. This in turn helps them to view themselves as bona fide dramatists.

If students want to experience the joys and agonies of being real playwrights, they have to see their work performed before some kind of an audience. This is the final test of ownership. Most schools publish students' poems and stories, and the publication of students' plays, though less common, is also a way of sharing the work—but performance, because that is what plays are meant for, is the best test for young playwrights, .

Graves is surely right when he says that publication should not be the privilege of a literary elite in the school, but should be available to all children as "an important mode of literary enfranchisement" (55). Yet to accomplish quality productions of every student's play is impossible. Production demands are enormous compared with those of publication. One solution is to hold a festival of selected plays one or more times a year. A less competitive alternative is to involve everyone in a group-written play (see chapter 5).

Both solutions aim to create a theatrical tradition in the school. Many levels and types of performance may be appropriate to the varied quality of the students' scripts. Impromptu readings in the classroom can lead to a more polished, rehearsed reading before other classes, and then to assembly programs, after-school drama clubs, full-scale school productions, and last but not least, professional presentations in a local or national young playwrights festival. There are more options than you might imagine that give young playwrights the chance to make mistakes at an early stage before experiencing those unpredictable joys and agonies of an ambitious production. I think it is good for writers to act in and direct their own work at least once, just to feel what their collaborators feel. But in the end, they have to sit and watch it with the rest of the audience. This can be very uncomfortable because one feels trapped. I remember an excellent piece of advice Stephen Sondheim once gave to some young playwrights. The occasion was an after-school group of sixteen- to eighteen-year-old dramatists that met with me on a weekly basis at the Dramatists Guild. Sondheim told them to watch their plays from the center of the audience, not from the back of the auditorium or the side of the stage. Only among the audience can you gauge their response: you both own the play and simultaneously feel it being taken away from you. Trust the performing arts to have contrived such a bittersweet, complex experience—but it is integral to the theatre, and teachers do young playwrights a disservice if they deny it them.

Response

Acquiring a feeling of ownership of one's writing can take a few years of steady practice. A crucial ingredient in achieving this sense is the supportive criticism of teachers and peers, but response means more than making judgments. In the early stages, it means being a good listener.

Young people, understandably enough, like someone to listen and pay attention to them. Sometimes this desire becomes obsessively self-centered and can smother their initiative and ability to function quietly on their own. This is familiar to all teachers and parents who try to educate children to take responsibility for and ownership of their lives. The more unfamiliar the task, however, the greater the need for reassurance. I remember the Pulitzer Prize winning dramatist Charles Fuller (*A Soldier's Play*), telling the same group of students Sondheim spoke to that he never showed any part of his script to anyone until he himself was pleased with it, which usually meant going through at least five or six drafts. His talk lasted a good hour, but of all things, it was this utter trust in his own standards that surprised and even shocked the group. Fuller was adamant about it, however, and I felt a sudden and simultaneous drain of confidence and surge of determination ebb and flow through this group of very talented and outwardly self-assured young people. The demands of professionalism frightened and challenged them. At the end of the evening, I still had the usual requests for me to read their latest additions, scenes, or drafts as a half-dozen insecure writers bunched around me, thrusting their manuscripts into my hands. It takes time for lessons like Fuller's to take hold!

Response and revision take time. Students will not revise if there is no time for the teacher and others to respond, so they will treat the first draft as the only draft. Perhaps they will compose a second draft by laboriously copying the first to make it look neat, but they will avoid making any real changes that may stimulate yet more changes and thus spoil the paper's appearance. Revisions become superficial and cosmetic. This is why students will prefer to erase a mistake rather than more quickly crossing it out and correcting it above or below the line or in the margin.

This is frustrating, because an important aspect of response is knowing what changes have been made and why. Graves says, "Children show us what they see in their writing when they change something. This is what revision is all about—seeing again. . . . If teachers are to help children control their writing, they need to know what children see, and the process and order of their seeing" (151). This applies to playwrights and writers of all ages. Sometimes I understand a new play that I am about to direct only if I get the chance to read an earlier draft of it. Understanding a writer's script means understanding the thinking that produced that script, which is why I urge people not to throw away discarded scripts or portions of a script. And that is why it is so useful for a teacher to read what has been crossed out as well as what has been left in.

If young playwrights have Time, Ownership, and Response, they are more likely to have a strong investment in their writing. They will revise their first drafts quickly and enthusiastically, because they will see the discrepancy between the subject they know so well and care so much about, and the words they have written. It is to that happy state of assertive, controlled playwriting that a teacher strives to bring his or her students.

Dramatic Language and Literary Convention

A penciled scrawl might mean something very complex to a child, but it remains meaningless to others. Ask the child to talk about it, and he or she will explain it in great detail. A sentence with no verbs or conjunctions will be crystal clear to the author, however incomprehensible it might be to the reader. Ask the author to read out the sentence, and he or she will either automatically supply the missing words, or the tone of voice will suggest them and make the meaning clear. This process of decoding writing through reference to speech is crucial. If students have limited writing skills, they may not have so many problems with their verbal skills, which is what playwriting depends upon—real voices speaking realistically.

As ways of creating and communicating meaning, writing and talking are completely different yet inextricably intertwined. For example, we refer to the distinctive quality of someone's writing as his or her voice. If we take this idea literally, we can ask students to verbalize their feelings and ideas as a first step toward clarifying them, then ordering them, and finally writing them down. The discussion and improvisation portions of a playwriting workshop are designed to give students confidence in writing plays by letting them first talk about them, then trying out their ideas by verbalizing them in an improvisation.

Writing a play has nothing to do with academic ability; it has even less to do with literary conventions, spelling, "correct" English, syntax, or grammar. If you think that playwriting will automatically help students to write correctly, forget it. Writing a play requires an awareness of and an interest in the life around and inside one. It is a social, not a literary, art. The person who gossips on the street corner is likely to have more flair for playwriting than the person who remains holed up in the library. A violent argument can produce more dramatic language, insults and all, than the most exquisitely phrased sermon. A playwright creates meaning primarily through dialogue. Observe something and find ways for people to talk about it—that is what the playwright does, and it is what we all do, from a very early age, by recounting our experiences, gossiping, arguing, telling stories, mimicking people we like or do not like, miming, or making different noises to communicate our meaning. All this happens before we starting writing expository prose, taking spelling tests, or learning about synonyms. Such literary skills certainly help a playwright communicate meaning, but they remain a tool, not a goal—and exercises in playwriting won't necessarily teach a writer literary skills.

Be careful not to impose the wrong literary standards on playwriting. What may appear to be an obsession with exclamation points or dialogue in a short story may in fact be the beginnings of a play. In *Lessons From a Child*, Lucy McCormick Calkins refers to two children's pieces of writing (see Figures 8–1 and 8–2) as follows:

> Diane used a steady stream of chitchat in her little stories. . . . she seemed unable to switch out of dialogue. . . . a certain inflexibility is apparent in many of Diane's third grade pieces. . . . I wondered if there was a connection between Diane's entrapment in chitchat and Birger's entrapment in sound effects and exclamation marks. (1983, 56)

Lucy Calkins's criticisms may be valid for these pieces as short stories, but the children's inability to "switch" out of dialogue should

Figure 8-1   Diane's Writing

the cat caper

I Was waching tv.   My father stad he had something for me.   I went
down stare's   "Watch out" "crash" "baing" "boom"!   ouch   you soupid
cat you soudin't of got in my way.   ya dad wat was that all about.
the stopid cat got in my way he stuk his hind leg out.   He opened the
drawer.   "Heres is yore gift—it's gone!"   I just saw kity run up stars
with it   let's get him.   let's be sneky About this   thar he is   he spotid
us   let's get him.   I fell like a polesman   you should   we are after
a crimiel!   there he is runig down the Hall.   I will get him.   "crash"
"baing"! Help......!   "boom"!   What hapied   I fell throw the florw
you supied dyit cat man striks agen.   We could of got him.   if that flor
Hadin't of caved in!

Figure 8-2   Birger's Writing

1) Wh, Wh, Wh you Brock my tooth Joyanny!
2) kh,kh, Oh, I felt my tooth fall out of my mouth!
3) Slam, Bang, Oh!

really signal to us that they are writing plays, not stories. The "chitchat"
is not as random as it seems: it is actually economic dialogue that tells
a story clearly. It has feeling, and it has a definite point of view. Similarly, Birger's entrapment in sound effect and exclamation points is
not necessarily an entrapment at all, but a perfectly natural feeling for
drama. Earlier in the book, Calkins quotes Birger's explanation of his
liberal use of exclamation points: "I was trying to add excitement."
She says that she and Birger then explored "alternative ways to add
excitement" (20). This surely misses the point. Birger's exclamation
points and sound effects are stage directions for a play. What Birger
wrote are snippets of dialogue that express feeling in action. They do
not describe a feeling, they dramatize it.

   Diane's title also gives us a clue to the dramatic mode she is in:
"The Cat Caper" sounds like a Marx Brothers farce or a Tom-and-Jerry
cartoon. If you were to act Diane's play with real clowning skill, you
would realize that what Calkins calls "a certain inflexibility" is in fact
an instinctive grasp for the disciplines of slapstick comedy. The focus
is entirely on the human reaction; the cat itself is hardly visible. This
fulfills one of the great rules of comedy: never concentrate on the
source; always focus on the reaction. A banana skin is not funny.

Someone slipping on it is. I maintain that Diane will never realize how real her story is, will never experience the emotional excitement she tried to invest in it, until its true form is recognized and revealed in performance. Diane's play-manque teaches us that dialogue, especially when it dramatizes rather than describes actions and feelings, is one of the best ways for children to test the quality of feeling and the emotional reality of their writing. Does the dialogue have a real "voice"? Can you hear it, feel it, experience it?

Bad Language

Reality should be the yardstick when judging matters of propriety, yet some teachers understandably get into a panic about profanity, obscenity, foul language, and even colloquialisms. Young people adopt their elders' standards and frequently object to what they feel is gratuitous swearing at a performance of a contemporary play. Then they return home and watch with apparent equanimity a TV show full of gratuitous violence.

A teacher will not solve society's double standards about freedom of speech in the classroom alone. The more often children see first-rate professional theatre, the more quickly they will adjust to the requirement of language in plays. If professional theatre is unavailable, plays should be read aloud in class. "Bad" language has to be confronted in a context where its use is clearly valid. Only then can the teacher lead the ensuing discussion with confidence. The most important objectives of such a discussion must be to encourage students to:

1. Take responsibility, as artists, for the language in their plays, and therefore learn how to become discriminating in their choices.
2. To understand that the moral values of their characters belong to the characters, not to the writer.

The most amazing and precocious example of the discriminating use of obscenity that I have ever read is in Juliet Garson's *So What Are We Gonna Do Now?* published in *The Young Playwrights Festival Collection* (1983). This play was performed in the 1982 Young Playwrights Festival, and is about two girls, both eleven, trying to deal with the sexual violence they encounter on the streets of Manhattan. They decide to dress up as prostitutes, entice all the perverts (or "sleazers," as they call them), and murder them. The burlesque style of this play cleverly distances the fear and loathing these two little girls feel whenever they want to play in their neighborhood, but the humor never undermines the seriousness of the situation. Their preposterous plot is hatched with venomous passion in a long and angry speech in which Jennifer imitates the disgusting sex talk she has to listen to:

JENNIFER: No, I left in such a rage this morning that I ran out without it. Now, you know whose fault this is, it's my mother's. If she's gonna drive me out of the house, she should at least have the courtesy to drive me out into a decent neighborhood. I mean, gosh, how can she expect me to grow up to be a normal human being, let alone an honest one, when look at the atmosphere she's set up for me. She's given me a choice, live in a house of distrust or go out into the streets of slime. The streets where scum drips drips from every man's mouth. *(Imitating various types of perverts)* "Hey, babe you know, ya beautiful." *(For this next type she puts her hand down near her you-know-what to make it look like a guy who's holding* his *you-know-what which is something they often do while they're speaking)* "Five more years little girl. Hey little girls, come' ere I got somethin' ta show you. Hey little girl, you evuh suck dick befo'? Jou want to come to my house? I take jou to da movies and buy jou candy." I swear! I can't go anywhere without hearing that junk! I can't walk on my block after dark without a car slowing down and following me. Stopping when I stop to tie my shoes. Because they think I'm a hooker! Me! A hooker! It makes me so upset. It makes me feel like *I'm* the disgusting one! Why should I feel disgusting because of their diseased minds?! I can't play in the park, I can't walk on my block, I CAN'T LIVE IN THIS WORLD ANYMORE! Wait a minute. I should be able to live in this world. *They're* the ones who shouldn't be able to. They want prostitutes! Prostitutes they'll get—and *DEATH*!

Notice the contrast between the angry voice of the character imitating the sex talk of the "sleazer" and the modest voice of the author in the stage direction. The action Jennifer describes is kept firmly off stage, but the report of it, in the words of an eleven-year-old, is just as shocking. With this device, the author has effectively dramatized an obscenity, without either lessening its impact or being offensive for no reason.

Dealing with this kind of subject matter and language in the classroom is not easy. The teacher has to try to shift students from the agenda of discipline to that of aesthetic judgment. This judgment is also controlled by the writer's, not society's, moral assessment. Although some students will abuse the freedom a teacher gives them in these matters, careful discussion will help them to become more discriminating and less anxious about the language they write for their characters.

9

Topic and Genre—
What Are They
Saying?

The importance of decoding students' writing also extends to decoding their choice of subject matter. Many of the scripts received for the Young Playwrights Festivals in both the United Kingdom and the United States are based on familiar models: TV soap opera, *Star Wars, ET,* gangster movies and thrillers, murder mysteries, and the occasional literary model such as absurdist and Pinteresque plays, or the more antique forms of drawing room comedy and Shavian debate. It would be easy to dismiss these plays as lacking authentic feeling, as empty of real meaning. It would also be wrong. The implication may be that the choice of topic is weak, that it is imitative of a favorite film or TV program, and that it debases or obliterates the author's "real" experience.

There is a real danger here. The Festival, both at the Royal Court in London and at the Circle Rep in New York, encouraged a certain attitude that consigned all these "imitative" plays, along with the vast majority of what passes for plays for children and young adults, to the inner circle of hell—escapist fantasy! I was as much to blame as anyone else. Indeed, I was more to blame, since I was in charge for much of the time. I think that because both the Royal Court and Circle Rep have built their reputations on two very different types of realism, the members of the Festival staff understandably looked for plays that fit into their own theatres' schema. We puritanically applied our own

preconceptions of realism and censored the children's writing accordingly: a gritty drama about life in the streets was more "real" and
"better" than a fantasy about a war in space or an extraterrestrial on
earth.

Adults continually apply double standards. No wonder children
get confused. It's OK for George Lucas or Stephen Spielberg to make
science fiction or fantasy films. It might be OK, or at least cute, for a
six-year-old to write about a monster, but it is not OK for a sixteen-
year-old to write a play about a monster. What I was doing to these
pieces of speculative drama—science fiction and fantasy—was wrong.
I refused to go beyond my immediate impression of the content. I
missed the students' meaning and intent because I was too busy imposing my own. I finally began to decode these plays just as Bettelheim
decoded fairy tales, and I finally began to enjoy them on their own
terms, just as we can enjoy *ET* on its own terms.

When students write gangster plays, thrillers, or space operas, they
are trying to recreate, primarily for themselves and only secondarily
for an audience, the emotional thrills they experienced watching the
original. This is no different from their writing about their experiences
at home, at school, on the football field, or the neighborhood streets.
In both cases, the writers are not trying to run away from their feelings,
but to realize and recreate them as vividly as possible.

You cannot blame students, therefore, for choosing the subject of
a movie because it excites them. When these students get discouraged
because their plays do not seem as exciting as *Star Wars*, you should
not necessarily shoo them away from the subject altogether. Teach
them how the subject can be made exciting, how to make the strong
feelings they have about the content real in the form of a play they
can write, rather than in the form of a major motion picture, which
they cannot. Keep faith with the student's personal impulse, however
imitative the subject may seem. Let's look at ways in which a teacher
can help students express their impulses in playwriting.

Earlier, I defined the voice of a writer in terms of dialogue that we
could hear, feel, and experience. If I apply this litmus test to the space/
gangster/monster plays, I quickly detect how clear or obscure the author's emotional investment is in the piece. If it is all action and no
dialogue (sound effects but no voice), the play will quickly degenerate
into a series of mechanical reactions, like a video or pinball machine.
Scene after scene will sound like this:

NEMO: Captain, there's a meteor storm dead ahead of us!
CAPTAIN: Action stations! Red Alert!
(Boom!)

The young author will complain that that is exactly what she en-
visaged in her play—the excitement of a Space Invaders game. It is

common for young people to despair at the technological crudeness of the stage in contrast with the" more real" excitement of film's sophisticated special effects. How does a teacher of playwriting keep faith with the personal impulse of an author who wants to write a play with the static emotional involvement of a video game?

The stage cannot communicate the tempestuous excitement of the unheard narrative running through a video game player's head. The teacher must show, by enacting the piece and thereby demonstrating the gap between what the author wants and what she has written, that the excitement of a play is contained in the reactions of the characters to a central event. The more involved we get with these reactions, the more dramatically exciting the event will be. One way of multiplying these reactions is to shift the point of view, to Ground Control, for example. Another way of building credibility is to concentrate on the story of one person, our hero or heroine. This personalizes a hitherto impersonal subject. Use the exercises on Dramatic Action and Character (chapters 2 and 3) to help the author invest her excitement in a form that is capable of expressing it.

It is important to decode the play's intention first before suggesting any particular strategy. If the young writer is excited by the technology of space exploration, encourage him or her to research the subject more thoroughly. The hero could then be an injured technician who must give the captain orders on how to repair the ship's main drive: status becomes defined by technical expertise. However, if the writer is more interested in the power that the hero wields in the face of overwhelming odds—destroying Space Invaders at the push of a button—then the play will concentrate on the authority, courage, and discipline he or she displays in rallying the crew for the final assault on the enemy. In other words, the preparations for the battle, not the battle itself (see Brian Way's *Development Through Drama* [1967] for other discussions along this same line). You might also suggest that the author use a heroine rather than a hero, and add interest to the story by challenging gender stereotypes.

Through careful discussion with young playwrights, a teacher can encourage students to articulate what they know about a subject, what they need to research, and what angle they can bring to it in order to fully express their emotional investment.

Research

A student's initial enthusiasm for a subject may evaporate once the surface glamour has to yield to more substantial investigation, in which case, he or she will probably choose a different topic. But research may also reinforce enthusiasm and provide the necessary details of specific places, times, and actions that the dramatic action requires. Research can also be fun and can involve several members of the class. Here are nine elementary school students from Moorestown, New Jersey, describing their approach to a group-written and group-performed play:

> We have been working on our play for several months, and have made puppets to go along with it. We made the main characters' heads out of plaster of paris and we made flats for the minor characters. We began by choosing interesting people from New Jersey. We chose Samuel Morse and Thomas Edison and did a lot of research on both of them. We have just recently performed it for our classmates and parents.

These children were authors, actors, prop-makers, costumers, dramaturgs, and by the end of it, I am sure, enthusiastic public relations staff for a theatre they invented and owned. Art and craft, along with history and language arts, supported their dramatic efforts. And their contribution to community awareness and education—how many people know that Morse and Edison came from New Jersey?—is also impressive.

The most impressive example of research I know is that done by a fourteen-year-old Ohio girl who became interested in the English Public School system. She read thirty-seven books, essays, and stories on the subject! Her play, *Epiphany*, took two years to write, contained forty-nine characters, was three acts long, and was set in 1912. It came to my attention through the 1981 Marilyn Bianchi Kids Playwriting Contest in Cuyahoga County, Ohio, and I produced a staged reading of it in the New York 1982 Young Playwrights Festival. It is a wonderful play and well worth reading. (It is available in *The Young Playwrights Festival Collection* [1983].) Not the least of its virtues is that its research is unobtrusive.

The fundamental lesson students need to learn about research is that imagination is not a blank check. It needs to be respected, like any scientific instrument. We all know you don't have to be an alcoholic to write a play about an alcoholic. You do not need to have gone through an abortion or a murder to write a play about abortion or murder. You use your imagination, but the imagination must be directed by observation, knowledge, and chosen point of view. All these things inform the author's enthusiasm and help guide his research. That is why I always urge young playwrights, and indeed, all writers, to keep a small notebook, small enough to slip into a pocket, so that notes can be made on the spot. All manner of seeming trivia can then be stored and used as raw material for play making. Use of a notebook trains playwrights in the art of observation and/or recording and interpreting such observations. I tell students that a playwright has to become a private investigator, like Sherlock Holmes, and make notes toward the completion of some master theory—a play! Tennessee Williams summed it up neatly in *Vieux Carre* when he refers to writers as "shameless spies."

Some students will choose remote and exotic settings for their plays without a real emotional investment. Two boys at Richmond Hill High School in Queens wrote about a cheese factory in Sweden in 1885, and two Spaniards in search of Kafka's tomb, lost in Czechoslovakia.

Neither boy was remotely interested in his ostensible subject, which was chosen in order to resist, rather than encourage, research. They were both trying to write an "absurdist farce." They wanted to impress the class with their originality, but their real investment was to make us laugh, and their model was Monty Python.

Comedy

Comedy depends on the seriousness of the characters' intentions even in the most ludicrous situation, with only the occasional self-awareness breaking through. What is funny is the logic of the situation, however crazy—not the overall oddity of the scenario. In structuring a play, be it drama or comedy, the same rules apply: Ask *why* things happen; dramatize the characters' status in relation to one another; show the argument. By treating the unfamiliar as if it were completely familiar, you can bring a point of view to bear on even the most unlikely subject!

Monsters and Ghosts

If farces are designed to make us laugh, monster plays are meant to frighten us. The crucial thing here is to focus, as in Diane's "The Cat Caper," on the human reaction, not on the monster itself. The best monsters are kept off stage, suggested only.

In *Psycho*, the notorious shower scene concentrates on the victim, with only occasional glimpses of a vague shape silhouetted behind the water or the shower curtain. The masks of Darth Vader and the maniac killer in *Friday The 13th* are also frightening because of their malevolent lack of features. The monster in *Forbidden Planet* is seen finally only as a vague outline. It is everyone's reaction to it that compels our own fear. No one has ever seen a monster, so everyone has a version of one based on what triggers certain reflexes. I know someone who is terrified of the thought of wet tea leaves touching his skin. The source of his terror may seem harmless to others, but it is very real to him. So whatever kind of monster a playwright chooses to invent, the trick is to concentrate on the human reaction first, thus encouraging empathy, and then bolster it with a sufficiently generalized or elemental symbol of fear, such as darkness, shadowy and indeterminate shapes, indistinct or distorted voices.

Discuss with the students what frightens them, reminding them that an audience can experience only what it can see and hear. It cannot feel. Discuss how horror is increased when placed in a context of calm or safety. Just when you thought it was safe to . . . Go swimming . . . Aargh! Take a shower . . . Aargh! Go on a picnic . . . Aargh!

The transformation of something from appearing normal into something abnormal can also be frightening, but the stage can rarely depict this transformation literally (one of the notable exceptions being the Theatre Sans Fil of Montreal, which performed a very frightening version of *Lord of the Rings*). The presence of deformity can be indicated simply in a shift of the body weight, as was done in the stage production of *The Elephant Man*. This mimed deformity was real to the other characters and therefore real to the audience. Everything depends on suggestion, not literalism—on feeding the imagination with just a bit of the fantasy monster, but with massive doses of human reaction to it.

Ghosts are different from monsters; they are much more versatile. They exist to warn, inform, or even comfort characters. Their initial presence may frighten, but if they stay around, they need to be treated seriously as characters. They need to be given goals, the same as any live character would be—What do I want? How do I get what I want? Ghosts can even represent an opposing point of view.

The invisible spirit with the mischievous sense of humor is a stock character in comedy. The fun depends on our seeing the mortal character made the victim of a number of disasters which to him are inexplicable and spooky. The author uses his planned audience reaction to create the effect he wants: if the audience sees Puck place the ass's head on Bottom, it laughs. It is sharing Puck's point of view. If the audience does not understand how Bottom is transformed, it remains perplexed, even frightened. It would then share Peter Quince's point of view. The clever playwright can manipulate an audience's feelings between these two extremes by adjusting how much we see or do not see. This shift between perceptions, from a human world to a ghostly one, is no different from exercises in shifting points of view discussed in the chapters on dramatic action and character. The primary purpose of these shifts is to understand more clearly the central action and the central character; ghost stories such as "A Christmas Carol" illustrate this point.

Fantasy

Sometimes, the borderline between fantasy and reality becomes very blurred, like a dream. Fantasy plays such as *Peter Pan* start off being firmly rooted in the human world. The flight into fantasy allows the characters to deal with real, human anxieties. The juxtaposition of the two worlds intensifies the experience of being alive for these characters, so much so that even death is considered an extension of the fantasy— an adventure. Far from an escape from real life, fantasy implodes into a person's experiences and reveals in greater detail the minute particulars of those experiences. Fantasy has its own logic, its own rules. It connects with something very powerful inside us. The terrors of a nightmare always disturb us because we wonder what connections they have with our conscious lives. The more extreme the fantasy or nightmare, the more profound the human disturbance.

Young people rarely write fantasy plays along the lines of *Peter Pan*. I think it is because they are struggling to deal with their conscious lives so much that they either suppress their fantasies or drag them into the light and make them part of their everyday living. Young adults are often aggressive about living their lives—sometimes to the point of death. They run headlong into life's most extreme and sensuous experiences, bruising themselves in the process. They are more ego-centered than most adults, especially during adolescence, when they feel the burden of the whole world pressing on their shoulders. They perceive less contrast between the ordinary and the fantastic because they are busy grabbing every fantastic opportunity from real life.

This kind of childhood and adolescence is extremely different from what it was a century ago. Plays like *Peter Pan* and books likes *Alice in Wonderland* and *The Water Babies* were written at a time when childhood was socialized as a special and distinct time in someone's life. Even the working-class children, who worked in the mines or in the chimneys, were sentimentalized in this literature. The child's role was so artificial that the only way his or her real life could be expressed was in fantasy.

This no longer applies. Children's literature today concentrates on the immediate social reality, and only in rare cases, such as Alan Garner and Madeleine L'Engle's superb novels, does a fantasy shift into a qualitatively different world. However, the world of today's children's theatre seems caught in its Edwardian roots. Even a cursory glance at the titles and subjects of most of today's children's and young adult plays reveals how different their topics are from those that interest students writing their own plays.

This is where we return to our theme of how to make plays real. Fantasy is a way of confronting and analyzing reality. It is not an escape from dirt and grime; instead, it is almost the essence of dirt and grime! The Alice in Wonderland is the *real* Alice, much more so than the little girl by the river. When children write plays they are struggling with their reality, trying to control it and contain it. They are not trying to rise above it. They are also trying to communicate it to other people. If what they write is a sham, it is because they have not adequately reflected on their work, or are trying to obey other people's standards of reality. Or it might be a sham because the child's investment was small, and the attempt to write on that topic proved to be less interesting than he or she had thought. Fantasy is going to be an ingredient in many student's plays anyway, because it is an obvious way in which the imagination can control the subject matter. If an author really wants to experience a space war and wants us to experience it as well, then the fantasy will be connecting powerfully with the main characters' needs. When the subject matter deals with experiences closer to home, the fantasy will be less other-worldly, but no less deeply felt, as in *What Are We Gonna Do Now*.

Teachers who bemoan the lack of fantasy in children's writing betray not only an idea of fantasy fixed in the nineteenth century, but a deafness to what the children are actually saying in their plays.

Summary

This chapter has argued that we should be aware of the danger of prejudging children's choices of topics. We should accept what children write and help them to see what they have written. Does it express what it was meant to express? Helping students reflect on their writing after the first draft and then helping them to improve it or to start again when a topic fails to be as interesting as they had hoped, will eventually train the class to think and write reflectively. They will respond to what they really want to write about. They will use their imaginations in more adventurous and nonliteral ways, rather than following the example of TV. As they develop their powers of reflection and judgment, they will develop a technique for dealing with the abstract concepts in dramatically concrete terms.

Students have many options in their choice of topic. If you can help them overcome the obstacles involved in choosing to write about gangsters/space wars/monster plays, you will be in a good position to guide students when they choose to write about more familiar, day-to-day experiences.

10

Why Teach Playwriting?

Any discipline that puts a great and ancient art form at the disposal of students, that will enable them to communicate more effectively, that encourages them to be more than just an audience, is worth teaching. Playwriting, drama, is one of the oldest and greatest of the art forms. This enfranchisement of students that drama can provide is the first, the most important reason for teaching playwriting. It is also one of the many reasons given for not teaching playwriting.

In Greek, the word *drama* means "action" or "deed." When the word relates to theatre, it means experiencing an action, living through it—and its consequences—as a means to understanding its significance. Drama's medium is the human being, created by the playwright, brought to life by the actor. Drama may *use* music and design, the whole array of theatrical technology and spectacle, but at its core, "good drama is made up of the thoughts, the words, and the gestures that are wrung from human beings on their way to, or in, or emerging from, a state of desperation" (Tynan 1957). *Wrung* is the key word here; it evokes drama's emotional impact, its gut level connection with our own lives. Even as drama necessarily distorts, formalizes, or even simplifies life, it still approximates, more closely than any other form, the texture of everyday living in all its "minute particulars." This insistence on detail is a good theatrical rule of thumb. The second reason for teaching playwriting, then, is that drama deals with human behavior in recognizable form and with the interaction of human emotions in real time. Drama is as immediate as life, but unlike life, it contains, more or less concealed, an organizing factor, a structure that can be recognized objectively only after the event or performance. The organizer is, of course, the dramatist.

Two more reasons to teach playwriting follow naturally. If we comprehend what happens in a play because of our emotional response to it, and only later objectively consider what we have seen, then drama's great power lies in the evocation of empathy, not merely sympathy. Drama does not let us stand to one side and feel for the characters; it drags us in so that we must feel with them. Drama encourages empathy with every conceivable character, from Danish princes to cunning infanticides like Medea, to Chaplin's ingenuous Little Tramp—so it must be communicating to us something very basic about human values. This is what makes drama so accessible to children who, from an early age, play "let's pretend" to learn about life.

To summarize then, the four great reasons for teaching young playwrights are

1. it is a great art form which students can use as a means of communication and entertainment,
2. it employs recognizable human behavior for its basic material,
3. it encourages empathy with human behavior in all its forms, and
4. it thereby promotes understanding of basic human values.

Some Misunderstandings

Before I offer any more reasons, let me clear up a common misunderstanding. Empathy means identification with and understanding of characters. It does not mean approval of their behavior. We share Medea's rage, her grief, her desire for vengeance—we do not approve of her actions. Nor can we dismiss her as either psychotic or an animal, as we might someone we read about in the newspapers. Dramatizing exemplary behavior is not how drama promotes understanding of human values. To do so would be didactic. Some people who write plays for children think that drama ought to teach in a pedagogical manner, like instruction in elementary arithmetic. This is an insult to children's intelligence. Children do not learn about life in such a way. Their play does have its own peculiar logic, as many experts have shown, but it can hardly be reduced to the simplistic formulas that much children's theatre (and I am afraid that much of it is appallingly second rate) seems to think it is. Plays are not pamphlets. They are not sermons. They must be as complex as life is, and only by being so can they remain true to life.

Different Points of View

This is not to deny that plays present opinions of their own or, rather, of their playwright. They may present many contradictory points of view while still offering an attempt at a balanced, overall view. Drama is moral, not because it teaches us how to behave but because it demonstrates a way of looking at life and demands that choices be made. It demands participation and decision. Playwriting helps students judge different points of view—not through casuistry, like television debates between polarized political opinions, but through credible dramatic, human action. Playwriting becomes, therefore, a tool for affective learning. As audience or playwright, one learns about a character by empathizing with it, standing in that character's shoes and speaking for him or her—that is what writing good dialogue entails. Each side must be real. The potential for learning here is obvious. Children learn about people's roles in life through precisely this kind of play. The roles we see enacted in child's play can and often do reflect adult prejudices, but the opposite can easily be the case. By dramatizing a completely opposing point of view, one may confront prejudice and promote greater understanding. What a tool for exposing hypocrisy and for challenging bogus thinking and sham values!

Use of Language

Realistic dialogue is a crucial ingredient in making dramatic action believable. It makes each point of view powerful enough to be accepted as a viable human argument. Literary dialogue, full of brilliant philosophizing, would be a disaster on stage because nothing depends on it—there is no dramatic action. There are always exceptions, of course— *My Dinner With Andre* is a notable one. But if it is human passion that compels our interest, it must be realistic. Drama is generally accessible because its verbal roots make playwriting a skill that may be mastered by someone with little or no formal education. Plays do not rely on spelling, syntax, or grammar. These formal skills, though important, must be seen as a means and not an end. They are of secondary importance to an intense awareness of what goes on around one. Language, in all its forms, from regional dialects to AMSLAN, expresses this awareness. The language must be part of the specific dramatic action; in turn, it must be supported by dramatic action. This is the only rule.

Playwriting itself does not teach "standard" English—but it is a superb tool for teaching students how language flexes itself and grows, shifts, and stretches. Students are more likely to learn this if a teacher first acknowledges that their verbal languages are valid in their own right and indeed are a treasurehouse to be plundered greedily. Initially, this may mean that some improvisations you conduct will contain "bad" language. Do not be put off by this, but look beyond it, and help the students discover new forms of verbalization that will release and harness their energies. What they are looking for is a way to express things that are important to them. You can provide them with the means. Teaching playwriting validates and enhances the students' own languages, whatever they are.

A Social Art

Teaching students to write plays helps us to discover what they are thinking and feeling. It also gives them the opportunity to explore and investigate unfamiliar worlds through dramatic fiction. We must be careful not to perpetuate the heresy of the fifties and sixties that the purpose of the arts in education was to encourage self-expression. Drama seeks to broaden, not limit. A play may start within the self; it may refer back to and *use* a playwright's own life experiences, but it will always go beyond the personal opinion or the strictly autobiographical to make a larger statement. An artistic statement is much richer and more complex than a reductionist view allows.

A play's statement is made very differently from a novel's or a poem's. It is less intimate. A play is a public expression of private thoughts. Drama is a social form that relies on the cooperation of many collaborators and exposure to some kind of an audience. The play's meaning must be exceptionally clear, as there is no turning back to reread a page. *Clear* does not necessarily mean *simple*; a good play will have people discussing it long after the curtain has fallen. Both the writing and the performance demand clarity, so the dramatist must exercise his or her imagination very carefully to fill in the details. Generalized descriptions of events (*"They stand on the corner chatting for a few minutes, then they decide to go to this bar. . . ."*) are impossible to stage, because performance requires specific, second-by-second choices. Nor can private thoughts or feelings remain private. Thus, "Mandy stayed in her room all day, not talking, because her mother had died," would be meaningless if translated to the stage. Dramatizing this action requires dramatizing the reaction to it: Mandy's absence provokes comment among her friends, and thereby excites the audi-

ence's curiosity. Playwriting challenges students' imaginations, and requires that they consider consequences. Seeing something in the mind's
eye is not enough.

This is a very courageous act. To encourage students in what is,
after all, a very scary undertaking, no matter how tantalizing, teachers
must abandon their role of "one who knows" —or rather, they must
reverse it and start from what the students know. Begin with their
viewpoint, their language. Don't hand them answers to their problems,
but free up their own ideas and then respond with your own viewpoint
to challenge them to look at things in a different way. This harnesses
the students' energies to question the status quo. Such a change of role
means being an artist alongside the students, learning to write plays
with them. This is not as difficult as it might at first seem: the roles of
teacher and artist share a similar sense of adventure.

Conclusion

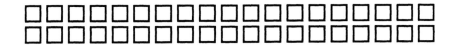

Strive for performance. However impromptu, performance tests the writing and validates the students' work as part of the dramatic tradition. If you treat their work with the same critical view and respect you bring to a professional work, you will enhance their sense of ownership of their writing. Performance will also teach students that the playwright's job does not end with the last sentence in the manuscript. Actors complement and sometimes challenge the writer's craft with their own. If the dialogue does not ring true, an actor can do nothing to make it convincing. During a workshop at Hunter Elementary School in Manhattan, a girl confided in Mary Rodgers, the workshop coleader, that "sometimes when I think it's the actors' fault that a scene doesn't play properly, it in fact turns out to be the fault of the scene itself." Mary turned to me and whispered, "A good notion to acquire early in one's career, methinks."

What you will be doing is teaching your students a form of communication, about the shape of language and verbalization. You will help them take what is familiar and make sense of it in an unfamiliar situation. They will learn to portray the unfamiliar with the same skill and detail as the familiar through a combination of imagination, research, problem solving, and development of an understanding of human behavior. If all this is just some of what drama encourages, who can call it elitist?

You will stimulate fresh thinking about "next year's school play." Some people will be reluctant to experiment with living young playwrights rather than dead old ones, but somewhere, sometime, people will begin to realize that, from the age of one onward, play investigates, expresses, and analyzes key life experiences through the safety of dramatic fiction. Far from being irresponsible and frivolous, drama can be a more flexible and useful tool for dealing with controversial issues than straightforward discussion, which can sometimes inhibit.

Teachers do make a difference. Otherwise, there would be no point in writing this book. Art should be accessible to all, and not merely to viewers or audience. Teaching playwriting is offering students a more useful form of empowerment than they might find on their own. With Eric Gill, that extraordinary artisan, thinker, and Catholic mystic, I believe that "an artist is not a special kind of person; everyone is a special kind of artist."

When I was in school, I flipped through a sculpture magazine, full of pictures of what looked like constructions of rubbish. I turned to my art teacher and said contemptuously, "But anyone can do this!" And he, bless him, replied, "Yes, and it's my job to get more people to do it." Quite—except that it took me fifteen years to understand what he meant. I now believe that teaching the arts to children and young adults brings with it the special delight of seeing people spring into them with the alarming abandon of the neophyte. They are just young enough not to have had to learn compromise, so they have less to lose, and occasionally strike home with frightening accuracy. We all know how little children have the habit of asking those awful, embarrassing questions; well, I think older children do the same, in a different way, with their playwriting. Adult playwrights sweat blood to recover that quality of radical candor which skewers injustice and pins it wriggling to the stage, often with hilarious results, yet with the weltschmerz that adolescence heaps on the young.

Remember, craft frees their instinct and honesty, and gives them a reliable, articulate voice. Craft unlocks that special kind of artist within each of us. The teacher can offer a way to that craft.

Bibliography

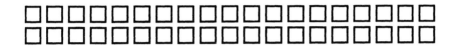

Theatre Games and Exercises

Barker, Clive. *Theatre Games*. London: Eyre Methuen Ltd., 1977.

> *For older students, this is a superb collection of games and exercises designed to help young actors tackle specific problems encountered in the study of drama.*

Johnstone, Keith. *Impro*. London: Eyre Methuen Ltd., 1981.

> *One of the finest books available on improvisations and theatre exercises, including valuable sections on Status and Narrative Skills. Enormously valuable to young playwrights.*

O'Neill, Cecily, Alan Lambert, Rosemary Linnell, and Janet Warr-Wood. *Drama Guidelines*. Portsmouth, NH: Heinemann Educational Books, 1977

> *A practical workbook of exercises in lesson form, easy for teachers to use.*

Scher, Anna, and Charles Verrall. *Another 100+ Ideas for Drama*. Portsmouth, NH.: Heinemann Educational Books, 1987

———. *100+ Ideas for Drama*. Portsmouth, NH: Heinemann Educational Books, 1975.

> *Two highly regarded books of exercises and ideas for drama. Full of useful ideas for young playwrights.*

Spolin, Viola. *Improvisation for the Theatre*. Evanston, IL: Northwestern University Press, 1963, 1983.

> *Spolin is the pioneer of the Theatre Games technique, which involves the wide use of improvisations to encourage the natural yet disciplined release of inner creativity.*

125

————. *Theatre Games for the Classroom.* Evanston, IL: Northwestern University Press, 1986.

This is a teacher's handbook with 150 of Spolin's Theatre Games, as well as notes and guidelines for teachers working with drama in the classroom.

Way, Brian. *Development Through Drama.* Atlantic Highlands, NJ: Humanities Press, 1967.

One of the classics in the field. Includes discussions of drama, as well as exercises designed to stimulate the creative imagination, improvisations, and exercises involving social drama. A very clear-eyed discussion of what makes a moment dramatic.

Writing and Playwriting

Calkins, Lucy. *Lessons from a Child.* Portsmouth, NH: Heinemann Educational Books, 1983.

Catron, Louis. *Writing, Producing, and Selling Your Play.* New York: Prentice Hall, 1984.

Catron is a prize-winning playwright, and in this highly readable and practical book, he discusses far more than just the day-to-day practicalities of playwriting. This is an accomplished and useful text for students who want to pursue their playwriting.

Graves, Donald. *Writing: Teachers and Children at Work.* Portsmouth, NH: Heinemann Educational Books, 1983.

One of the most inspiring and informative books written on the subject of children's writing and what both teachers and students learn from the process. A book for teachers—all teachers.

Pike, Frank, and Thomas G. Dunn. *The Playwright's Handbook.* New York: Plume (New American Library), 1984.

Like the Catron book above, this is both practical and inspirational. It looks at the step-by-step process of constructing a play, surveys the perils and pitfalls, and offers solid practical advice on how to live as a playwright.

Richards, Gillian, and Ray Sweatman, eds. *Dramatists Sourcebook.* New York: Theatre Communications Group, 1988.

This book deals with survival as a playwright and will serve to demonstrate to young playwrights all that playwriting entails. It has detailed listings of grants available, prizes offered, and theatres that produce new works. This is an invaluable source for the serious writer—and interesting reading for others.

Tynan, Kenneth. "Desperation." London: McGibbon and Kee, 1957.

Drama Education

Haseman, Brad, and John O'Toole. *Dramawise.* Portsmouth, NH: Heinemann Educational Books, 1986.

This is a classroom text offering a full drama course that leads to the students' creating their own dramas. Presents students with the basic concepts, forms, and structures of drama and puts these to work throughout in imaginative and challenging exercises.

McCaslin, Nellie. *Creative Drama in the Classroom.* New York: Longman, 1984.

Dr. McCaslin is one of the most respected authorities in the field of creative drama. This is a vital book for all teachers who want to learn more about and do more with drama in the classroom.

Morgan, Norah, and Juliana Saxton. *Teaching Drama.* Portsmouth, NH: Heinemann Educational Books, 1987.

This is a basic book for every drama teacher, a practical useful guide to the skills involved in teaching drama. It addresses the questions many teachers, experienced and inexperienced, have regarding the actual mechanics of using drama in the classroom.

Neelands, Jonothan. *Making Sense of Drama.* Portsmouth, NH: Heinemann Educational Books, 1984.

This concise "guide to classroom practice" offers teachers sound advice and encouragement on such aspects of teaching drama as "The Teacher-Learner Partnership," "Ways of Working," and "Planning Structure." Inherent in its sample exercises are implicit lessons on dramatic structure and internal logic. Its greatest value lies in its being a solid overview on how to approach drama with students.

O'Neill, Cecily, and Alan Lambert. *Drama Structures.* Portsmouth: Heinemann Educational Books, 1982.

This manual provides lesson plans and scenarios on different themes, offers teachers notes on some practical teaching problems, and possible avenues for further exploration. Suitable for both specialists or non-specialists. Easy to use, but consistently challenging.

Swartz, Larry. *Dramathemes.* Portsmouth, NH: Heinemann Educational Books, 1988.

A good, basic guide to drama teaching, with basic creative exercises and improvisations that can be developed further, into longer scenes and short plays. Primarily for teachers of younger students.

From the Young Playwrights Festival

Foundation of the Dramatists Guild. *The Young Playwrights Festival Collection.* New York: Avon, 1983.

Lamb, Wendy, ed. *Meeting the Winter Bikerider and Other Prize-winning Plays from the 1983 and 1984 Young Playwrights Festivals.* New York: Dell, 1986.

———. *The Ground Zero Club and Other Prize-winning Plays from the 1985 and 1986 Young Playwrights Festivals.* New York: Dell, 1987.

———. *Sparks in the Park and Other Prize-winning Plays from the 1987 and 1988 Young Playwrights Festivals.* New York: Dell, 1989.

Plays

Strindberg, August. "The Ghost Sonata." In *Plays One: Strindberg*, translated by Michael Meyer. London: Methuen, 1976.

————. "A Dream Play." in *Plays Two: Strindberg*, translated by Michael Meyer. London: Methuen, 1982.

Fuller, Charles. *A Soldier's Play*. New York: Hill & Wang, 1982.

Plays by and for Young Playwrights

Bass, Molly, and Sylvia Hoffmire. *The Painted Face*. Boston: Baker's Plays, 1989.

Bass, Molly. *Two To Go*. Boston: Baker's Plays, 1987.

Molly Bass won the 1986 Scholastic Writing Award for a dramatic script for The Teen Age, *published in* Two To Go, *which was produced at New York's American Place Theatre. Her view of teenage life, though lighter than some, is still presented honestly and dramatically. Her second play,* The Painted Face, *looks at teenage suicide—before the fact.*

Dee, Peter. *Voices from the High School*. Boston: Baker's Plays, 1982.

————. *. . . and stuff . . .* Boston: Baker's Plays, 1985.

Peter Dee's Voices from the High School *has for the past four years been on Dramatic Magazine's list of the ten most produced plays among U.S. high schools. Its honesty and unwillingness to tread softly among the real issues facing today's teenagers has earned it a lot of praise and condemnation, including one production's being banned by a school department. The students went on to perform it "underground"—off school property, without the support of the administration, but with the support of many of the teachers and parents.*

Erhard, Tom, ed. *Laughing Once More*. Woodstock, IL: Dramatic Publishing Company, 1986.

Louisville's Young Playwrights. *In Sight*. Woodstock, IL: Dramatic Publishing Company, 1986.

Lynn, Jess, et al. *Thirteen Heavens and Nine Hells*. Boston: Baker's Plays, 1988.

Many-Young-Playwrights, Walden Theatre Conservatory. *Glimpses*. Woodstock, IL: Dramatic Publishing Company, 1982.

————. *Rites*. Woodstock, IL: Dramatic Publishing Company, 1986.

————. *Inside Out-Upside Down*. Woodstock, IL: Dramatic Publishing Company, 1986.

Scanlan, Michael. *Inside/Out*. Boston: Baker's Plays, 1984.

————. *Candid*. Boston: Baker's Plays, 1986.

————. *Fortress*. Boston: Baker's Plays, 1988.

Michael Scanlan's plays are all collaboratively written with his high school students. They're all powerful plays looking at the life of young people today. Inside/Out is a collection of three one-acts. The title play looks at the external and internal perceptions of kids today: how they see themselves, how they would like to see themselves, and how others want to see them. Who? is a terrifically powerful piece about the struggle for identity, centered around the now infamous Who concert at Cincinnati's Riverfront Stadium. That Day deals with the pressures on students to be "important." Candid, a one-act play, looks at the break-up of a family through the eyes of T.J., a young photographer, after his mother walks out. Fortress is available both as a one-act and a full-length. It chronicles the lives of two students struggling to maintain their individuality and to get in with the popular kids.

Young Playwrights of the Walden Theatre Conservatory. *Sometimes I Wake Up in the Middle of the Night.* Woodstock, IL: Dramatic Publishing Company, 1986.